THE ISLANDS SERIES

THE SEYCHELLES

THE ISLANDS SERIES

* Published in the United States by Stackpole
† Published in the United States by David & Charles

THE
SEYCHELLES

by GUY LIONNET

DAVID & CHARLES : NEWTON ABBOT

STACKPOLE BOOKS : HARRISBURG

This edition first published in 1972
in Great Britain by David & Charles (Publishers) Limited
Newton Abbot Devon
in the United States by Stackpole Books
Harrisburg Pa.

ISBN 0 7153 5713 1 (*Great Britain*)
ISBN 0 8117 1514 0 (*United States*)

*Set in eleven on thirteen point Baskerville
and printed in Great Britain
by Clarke Doble & Brendon Limited Plymouth*

To Maxime Ferrari,
a Seychellois par excellence

CONTENTS

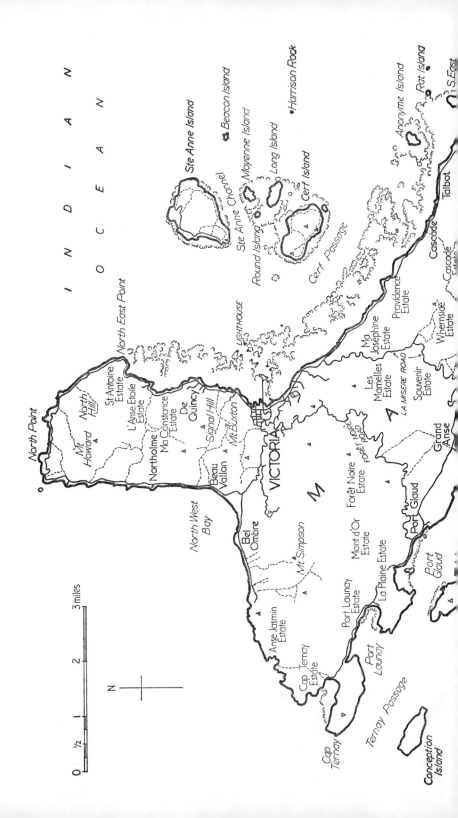

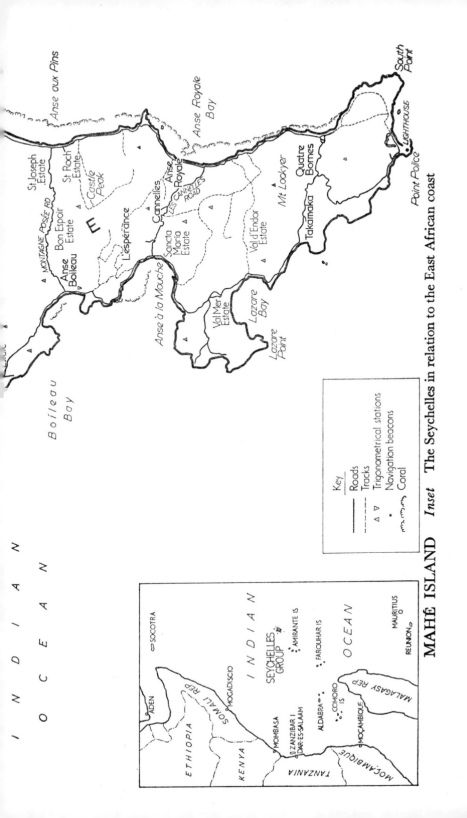

MAHÉ ISLAND *Inset* The Seychelles in relation to the East African coast

ILLUSTRATIONS

ILLUSTRATIONS

MAPS

Grateful acknowledgement is made by author and publishers to the following for permission to use the above photographs :

The British Overseas Aircraft Corporation, the Central Office of Information, London, Mr C. J. Piggott, Mr H. J. Schlieben and, lastly, Imprimerie St Fidèle, Victoria, who supplied all the photographs without credits shown above

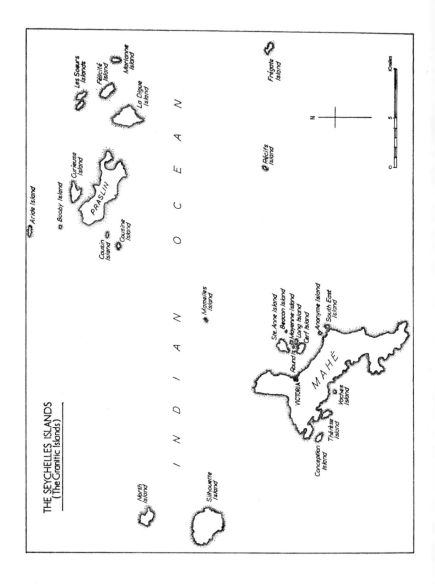

THE SEYCHELLES ISLANDS
(The Granitic Islands)

INDIAN OCEAN

North Island

Silhouette Island

Aride Island

Booby Island

Cousin Island

Cousine Island

Curieuse Island

PRASLIN

Les Sœurs Islands

Félicité Island

Marianne Island

La Digue Island

Mamelles Island

Frégate Island

Récifs Island

Conception Island

Thérèse Island

VICTORIA

Vaches Island

Ste. Anne Island

Round Island

Beacon Island

Moyenne Island

Long Island

Cerf Island

Anonyme Island

South East Island

MAHÉ

N

0   5   10 miles

1   GEOGRAPHY, GEOLOGY AND GOVERNMENT

THE most beautiful approach to the Seychelles is by sea. The mountains of the island of Mahé tower above the port of Victoria as the steamer passes the smaller islands of Silhouette, Praslin and La Digue before dropping anchor in the harbour. Launches and lighters then come alongside to take off passengers and cargo. The new international airport will no doubt be the arrival place for more and more of the increasing tourist traffic, but arrival by air will never match the excitement of being put ashore by launch with the smell of copra and cinnamon bark in the soft tropical air.

The port of Victoria is the Seychelles' only town and houses the colony's main public buildings as well as one quarter of the fifty thousand population. Yet it is only a tiny part of the Seychelles—a group of islands offering an intriguing variety of landscape and character.

GEOGRAPHY

The Seychelles are usually described as being situated between 4° and 5° S and 55° and 56° E, that is in the middle of the Western Indian Ocean at 575 miles (932km) from Madagascar, 980 miles (1,568km) from Mauritius, 990 miles (1,584km) from Mombasa and 1,748 miles (2,797km) from Bombay. This area includes only the central, mountainous granitic islands and three small coral islands which constituted the original Seychelles, and does not cover the outer, flat, coral islands, which form part of the

13

Seychelles today and are scattered in a long trail between the equator and Madagascar.

Originally, the Seychelles consisted of the granitic islands; of two small coral islands, Bird, or Ile aux Vaches, and Denis, which are on the northern edge of the Seychelles plateau, and the Plate island, a small isolated coral island south of the plateau. In 1903 when the Seychelles ceased to be dependencies of Mauritius and became a separate British Crown Colony, the other coral islands, except for Coëtivy and Farquhar, were also attached to the Seychelles. Coëtivy and Farquhar were detached from Mauritius and added to the Seychelles in 1908 and 1932 respectively. Desroches of the Amirantes group, Farquhar of the Providence group and Aldabra, of the Aldabra group, were transferred from the Seychelles in 1965 to constitute with the Chagos group (dependencies of Mauritius) the new British Indian Ocean Territory.

Mahé and the other granitic islands spring from a large crescent-shaped, shallow (forty fathoms deep) submarine plateau and stand in four close groups: Mahé and its ring of satellite islands; Silhouette and North island; the Praslin group and the small Frégate island and its islet. Between these groups are the rocky Les Mamelles, which looks like two rugged breasts, and Récifs island. The proximity, small size and steepness of these islands are best expressed in figures. There are respectively fourteen miles (24·4km), twenty-four miles (38·4km) and thirty miles (51·2km) between the main island of Mahé and Silhouette, Praslin and Frégate. Mahé is 36,200ac (14,480ha) in area and rises up to 3,000ft (914m) at the Morne Seychellois. The next island in size, Praslin, is 9,700ac (3,500ha) in area and its highest peak is 1,281ft (427m) high. Silhouette, which is the third largest, is 4,000ac (1,960ha) in area and its highest peak, Morne Dauban, is 2,600ft (867m) high. The other islands and islets, some of which are mere rocks, are much smaller, but have in general the same forbidding topography.

In contrast, the coral islands are spread over a much larger area and are only a few feet above the sea level. For the sake of convenience these islands may be divided into six groups. The first and nearest to the granitic islands consists of the small Bird island, or Ile aux Vaches, and Denis island which are fifty-two miles (83·2km) north of Mahé and are the only coral islands to be found on the extensive, 650 miles (1,040km) long, edge of the Seychelles plateau. The next group consists of two isolated islands, Plate island, which is about seventy-eight miles (124·8km) south of Mahé and is one of the smallest sand cays of the Colony, and Coëtivy island, which is twenty-five miles (40km) further south and is the largest Seychelles sand cay. The other groups, those of the Amirantes, Alphonse, Providence and Aldabra, lie roughly to the south-west and are respectively 145 (232km), 230 (368km), 390 (624km) and 600 miles (800km) from Mahé.

With a total area of some 107 square miles, the Seychelles are thus made of forty tall granitic islands and islets, occupying eighty-five square miles, and of forty-three low coral islands and islets, with an aggregate area of only twenty-two square miles.

The islands of the Western Indian Ocean include granitic islands, volcanic islands, sand cays and elevated reefs. All these types, except the volcanic islands, occur in the Seychelles.

If there is little difficulty in explaining how the coral islands of the Seychelles came into existence, it is much harder to explain the origin of the granitic islands.

The Granitic Islands

The granitic islands are made of continental rocks and have also a continental base. As is the case with all true continental formations, the Mohorovicic discontinuity, which separates the crust of the earth from its mantle, is twice as deep beneath these islands as it is beneath the surrounding ocean. They are, therefore, a striking exception to the rule that all oceanic islands are either volcanic or coralline. Various hypotheses have been put forward to try to explain this anomaly. The earlier ones, based

15

on biological evidence, claim that the Seychelles were once united with Africa and Asia by continental bridges or isthmian links. But, according to Alfred Wegener's original continental drift theory, the Seychelles would be fragments of Africa which were torn away when Gondwanaland disrupted and Asia separated from Africa to drift eastward. More recent hypotheses hold that the Seychelles are remnants of a micro-continent or of an ancient coast of Africa, which in the past extended much further east. Whatever may have been the case, geomorphologists generally agree about the existence up to the beginning of the Tertiary Period of a large land mass of some 50,000 square miles on the site of the present Seychelles plateau, which may have been the legendary Limuria.

The rocks of the granitic islands consist of the Precambrian, 600 million years old, granites of the Mahé and Praslin groups, the probably equally old aplites of Frégate and the Early Tertiary, 50 million years old syenites, of Silhouette and North Island.

Three main types of granite are distinguishable in the Mahé and Praslin groups: the Mahé grey granite, the grey and faintly gneissole granite of Ste Anne, Cerf and three other small islands east of Port Victoria and the reddish granite of Praslin and La Digue. All three have a similar composition, consisting of micro-perthite, quartz, oligoclase, minor amphibole and occasional biotite. The commonest intrusions in these granites consist of dark coloured, fine grained dykes of olivine dolerites and dolerites which are few inches to thirty feet wide and are found in the principal tension joints of the main granite bodies. They are particularly numerous on Félicité island, near La Digue. Facies of porphorytic granite and granite porphyry exist on the west coast of Mahé and extend to the neighbouring islands of Thérèse and Conception. Intrusions of granite porphyry occur also on Praslin. Marianne island, near La Digue, consists of granite porphyry. Aplite veins are also found on Praslin, La Digue and on other small islands of the Praslin group. Pure quartz veins are common on Praslin and on the neighbouring islets and are also numerous on the summit ridge of Aride island.

16

Page 17 Victoria, the capital of the Seychelles, and the only town: (above) seen from Signal Hill; (below) Royal Street, one of the main streets of Victoria, where are the Central Police Station and lawyers' and notaries' offices

Page 18 Victoria: (above) Government House, residence of the Governor and Commander-in-Chief of the Seychelles, built in 1911; (below) L'Horloge or Clock Tower, the best known feature of the town, was erected in 1903 in memory of Queen Victoria. It is a small replica of the Clock in Vauxhall Bridge Road, London

Frégate island differs markedly from the other granitic islands in consisting largely of aplite and granite porphyry, with only minor patches and veins of granite. Ilot, near Frégate, is however granitic.

Silhouette and North island consist of a buff to grey syenite with a somewhat variable composition. The commonest is a dark grey rock. Since syenite contains little or no quartz, quartz gravel deposits, which are so common on most of the granitic islands, are not present on Silhouette and North island. The syenite of these two islands is cut by dark coloured dykes and veins of porphorytic microsyenite.

Along the creeks and bays of the granitic islands are also found long, narrow calcareous plains, which are locally called 'plateaux'. They are seldom more than half a mile wide and extend from the sea shore to the base of the foot hills, from which they are often separated by small alluvial swamps. These coastal plains consist of coral and other marine debris and are relatively young, being some 3,000 years old.

The soils of the granitic islands consist of a tropical red earth or latosol, rocky and bouldery land, river valley land, marsh land, mangrove swamp and shioya. The most fertile of these are the small patches of river valley land and drained swamp land. The most important, however, is the slightly acid red earth which occupies a very large area of the granitic islands and is relatively fertile when uneroded, and the shioya of the coastal 'plateaux', which is a slightly alkaline, sandy and hungry soil, but bears the best coconut plantations of the granitic islands.

The Coral Islands

As with other islands of this kind, the coral islands of the Seychelles must have been formed, according to Darwin's theory, from coral reefs which grew on slowly subsiding volcanic submarine mounts and are made either of coral sand and other marine detritus which have accumulated on a base of dead coral reefs, or of reefs which have suddenly been raised above the level of the sea. They stand on shallow banks, like the Amirantes and

Alphonse banks, on ridges, like the Providence ridge, or rise individually from great depths, like the islands of the Aldabra group. The first type consists of the sand cays and the second of the rocky elevated reefs. Both types have been transformed by the weather, the sea, vegetation and animals, especially sea-birds.

The sand cays are of relatively recent formation, being some three thousand years old, and low-lying and generally sandy. One of them, Coëtivy, has small dunes. Most of them contained bird guano, now almost completely exploited, and contain hard phosphatic sandstones. The guano occurred as surface and underground deposits. The sandstones occur as nodules, loose blocks or as a deep and compact formation which may reach a depth of seven feet, especially towards the centre of the islands. Both the guano and the sandstones have been formed by the interaction of the calcium carbonate of the coral sand and of the phosphorus of the droppings of the large numbers of sea birds which are believed to have taken refuge in the Southern Indian Ocean sometime during the last glacial age. Beneath the sandy soil, floating on the saline water table which fluctuates with the tide, and slightly above the sea level, is the only fresh water of these islands. It occurs as a layer of Ghyben-Hertzberg lens, which mixes only slowly with the saline water because its rate of flow is limited by its slow penetration of the soil and because it is replenished by rainfall. The sand cays of the Seychelles comprise Bird, Denis, Plate, Coëtivy and the islands of the Amirantes, Alphonse and Providence groups. With a total area of a little less than 5,000ac (2,000ha), they consist of extensive coconut plantations which produce a substantial part of the crop of the Colony.

The uplifted reefs consist of solid corals, still in their position of growth, which have been raised a few feet above the level of the sea. There is little or no soil on these islands. The ground consists of hard, sharp, coralline limestone, with deep potholes. This formation is due to erosion by the sea and the rain on the exposed, metamorphosed reefs. The effect of the sea bird droppings has been much greater on these islands than on the sand cays. Indeed, the uneven leaching of the droppings in the cracks and holes of the original reefs has produced an uneven interaction between their phosphorus and the calcium carbonate of the reefs. As a result, all or the larger part of the interstitial, unmetamorphosed calcium carbonate has been weathered, leaving behind the hard and only slowly weatherable calcium phosphate in the form of sharp, jagged edges and pinnacles. The uplifted reefs are much older than the sand cays, being probably of the same age as the 150,000 year old fossil corals which are found under granite boulders, up to thirty feet (ten metres) above the sea level on the granitic islands.

Sand dunes exist on some of the larger islands, such as Assumption and Cosmoledo. Because of the porous nature of the ground there is no fresh water lens above the water table on these islands; the only fresh ground water to be found occurs in isolated wells— large, deep pot-holes in which rain water has collected. The elevated reefs comprise the most distant islands of the Seychelles, those of St Pierre, Assumption, Astove and Cosmoledo, with a total area of just under 5,500ac (2,200ha). They are covered with a spiny, stunted vegetation. Some of them used to be important breeding grounds for the green or edible turtle. Except for their guano these islands have little agricultural or industrial value.

The soils of the coral islands are all derived from coral and other marine detritus. They constitute the shioya, Farquhar, Desnoeufs and Jemo series. They are characterised by their high content of calcium carbonate, their sandy nature and slight alkalinity. The best and most extensive of these soil series is the shioya.

CLIMATE

The newcomer to the Seychelles is impressed not only by the hot and moist tropical atmosphere, but also by the equable temperature, the uniformly long day and night and by the short dawns and twilights. These are, of course, due to the proximity of the sea and to the islands' equatorial or sub-equatorial position. Still more remarkable, however, are the reversible monsoons of the land-locked Indian Ocean, on which the climate of the Seychelles is so dependent.

Two monsoons blow over the islands, the south-east from May to October, and the north-west from December to March, with November and April as transitory months. The south-east monsoon, with strong trade winds, is cool and dry while the north-west monsoon, which is generally calm, is hot and rainy. Both winds are produced by the permanent belt of high pressure which exists over the Southern Indian Ocean and which is especially prevalent during the southern winter, and by seasonal changes in pressure over the central massif of Asia. This passes from a belt of low pressure extending over North-West India and South-East Arabia during the northern summer, to a large anti-cyclone over the interior of that continent during the northern winter. On reaching the Equator and after passing the Seychelles, the south-east monsoon, owing to the deviating effect of the rotational movement of the earth, veers to the south and then to the south-west and is blowing in that direction when it reaches Peninsular India. It produces copious rainfalls from the large amount of moisture which it has gathered over the Indian Ocean.

The north-west monsoon consists of north-easterly winds which blow towards the sea from the Indian peninsula, but which also because of the effect of the earth's rotation backs first to the north and then to the north-west on passing the Equator. These winds are not as steady or as strong as those of the south-east monsoon and also have a much more limited course, since there is no large land mass to warm up the atmosphere and to intensify air circulation in the Southern Indian Ocean. As a result, the north-west monsoon does not blow much farther south than the Seychelles.

To the Seychellois the south-east monsoon, or *Suette*, consists of strong, fresh and dry winds which blow night and day for some four months of the year, when the sea is choppy, the sky dull and fish scarce. But it brings back millions of terns to the egg islands,

22

from which schooners load thousands of boxes of bluish, prettily spotted eggs for the food markets. The north-west monsoon, or *Vents d'Nord*, except for rare squalls which stir up the sea and blow down coconut palms and banana plants, produces calm, torpid days and nights which dissolve suddenly into torrential showers that obscure the sky and flush down the islands.

Rainfall varies from island to island. It tends to decline from the granitic islands to the southernmost coral islands. The mean annual rainfall at sea level on Mahé and Silhouette is 2,335mm (92in) and is probably of the order of 3,810mm (150in) at their highest points. On the lower islands of Praslin and La Digue and on the coral islands the mean annual rainfall becomes progressively lower, ranging from 1,770mm (70in) at sea level on Praslin and La Digue, to 1,700mm (67in) on Denis island, on the edge of the Seychelles plateau, 1,500mm (59in) on Daros island, of the Amirantes group, and 1,320mm (52in) on Alphonse. Monthly fluctuations follow much the same pattern on all the islands, although they tend to be more marked on the outer and drier islands. A large proportion of the rain, over thirty-three per cent, falls in heavy downpours during December, January and February. But only six per cent falls during the driest months of July and August. Rainfall decreases progressively from March to August and increases again from September. The extremes of rainfall recorded at sea level at Victoria, on the island of Mahé, are 3,684mm (145·06in) in 1934 and 1,237mm (48·72in) in 1943.

The mean annual temperature varies from 24° C (75° F) to some 30° C (86° F) at sea level, but is, of course, lower on the higher hills of the granitic islands. The daily temperature seldom exceeds 32° C (89·6° F) and rarely drops below 22° C (71·6° F) at sea level.

As the relative humidity is high, averaging seventy-five to eighty per cent all the year round, the coolness of the south-east monsoon, which brings the most pleasant time of the year, is therefore due mainly to its fanning effect rather than to a fall in temperature. Fortunately the Seychelles islands, except for the three southernmost ones of Providence, Cosmoledo and Astove, lie outside the cyclone belt of the Southern Indian Ocean and are spared the storms from which more southern islands, like the Mascarenes, periodically suffer.

DIFFERING ASPECTS OF THE ISLANDS

The Seychelles have been described as great jutting peaks rising blue-green out of a brilliant sparkling sea. These peaks are of course the granitic islands which can be compared with the mountain tops of a great sunken land. The coral islands, even the uplifted reefs, are flat white expanses on this same sea.

The Tall Islands

The apical aspect of the granitic islands is enhanced by their rockiness. Boulders, or 'glacis', abound on the islands, from the top of the highest mountains to the sea level. As there has been no volcanic eruption near or on the granitic islands, they have retained their original silhouettes. But time has left its mark, especially on the exposed rock surfaces, which bear long corrugations and have at some time been carved into fantastic shapes.

The granitic islands are thus steep and rugged mountainous masses whose peaks occur in ridges running along the longer axes of the islands. Numerous lateral spurs divide the islands into long and rather narrow stretches. This compartmentation, coupled with the relatively small area of arable land, has resulted in 'patchy' agriculture. Out of a total of some 55,000ac (22,000ha) there are only 2,500ac (1,000ha) of arable land; 25,000ac (10,000ha) of land suitable for tree crops, and 11,000ac (4,400ha) of forest land. The rest, some 18,000ac (7,200ha), consists of boulders and other surfaces unsuitable for agriculture.

Although well watered, the granitic islands have no rivers but have numerous streams running swiftly into the sea. Water catchment is therefore not easy and droughts, even short ones, produce water shortages.

The overall aspect of these islands, with their lush tropical vegetation, is that of high hanging gardens overlooking silver white beaches and clear lagoons.

All along the coast of the main islands are small villages, many of them fishermen's, made up of thatched cottages, often built on rocks piled up on each other, and nestling around a church and facing the sea. They have retained their old French names, such as Glacis, Bel'Ombre, Port Glaud, Anse Boileau, Anse à La Mouche, Anse Aux Poules Bleues, Baie Lazare, Takamaka, Anse Bougainville, Anse Royale, Anse Aux Pins, Pointe Larue, Cascade, Mamelles and Anse Etoile on Mahé, Grand'Anse and Baie Ste Anne on Praslin and La Passe on Silhouette and La Digue. Most of the rural population lives on the coast and along the coastal roads which now link even the most remote part of the islands. On the small islands there are only isolated cottages near the beaches.

The only town, Victoria, the old Etablissement du Roi of the French, is situated on the east coast of Mahé, with a small but good port, protected by a ring of islands and islets. It is made up of the Long Pier or La Chaussée, aptly called La Promenade des Créoles, since it is still the only Sunday 'promenade' of the town. At right angles to it are the coastal Victoria and Albert Streets, from which branch, again at right angles, the old, narrow, colourful Market Street, the new La Misère trans-island road, which leads to the west coast of Mahé, and the Royal Street and Duke of Edinburgh Way. The latter leads to the residential areas of Bel'Eau and Bel Air and runs on to another new trans-island road, Forêt Noire, which leads to the north-west of Mahé. Royal Street meanders over St Louis hill to join with the old Beau Vallon trans-island road, which leads to the Beau Vallon beach.

Of a total population of some fifty thousand, some forty-five thousand live on Mahé, and thirteen thousand of these have their homes in Victoria. Praslin, La Digue and the neighbouring islets have a total of some six thousand inhabitants. Silhouette, the third island in size, has less than a thousand. The other granitic islands have less than a hundred each. The coral islands, where

25

there is no permanent establishment, have a total population of about a thousand.

The Low Islands

Although the coral islands all look very much alike from a distance, they vary considerably in shape and size. Some of them, such as Poivre, St Joseph, Alphonse, Bijoutier, Providence, Cosmoledo and Astove, are atolls. The rest are single islands with fringing reefs. Among the atolls Astove is the only one with a virtually complete land rim. The other atolls consist either of a ring of islands, like St Joseph and Cosmoledo, or of single islands, like Poivre, Alphonse and Providence, emerging from an ancient eroded atoll rim.

The coral islands are spread over an area of some 400,000 square miles. The islands closest to the granitic islands, Bird and Denis, are 52 miles (83·2km) north and north-west of Mahé respectively. The most distant island, Assumption, is 622 miles (995·2km) west south-west of Mahé. The Amirantes, which are the main group of sand cays, is an average distance of 143 miles (228·8km) south-west of Mahé. The uplifted reefs of St Pierre, Cosmoledo, Astove and Assumption are the most distant islands.

The islands vary in size from the very small banks of St Joseph atoll, which measure only a few acres to Assumption island which has an area of 2,735ac (1,094ha) and is the largest coral island of Seychelles. The next island in size is the sand cay Coëtivy, with 2,293 ac (917·2ha). The medium size islands of Denis, Daros, Poivre, Alphonse, Providence and St Pierre vary from 275ac (110ha) to 430ac (172ha) in area. The smaller islands comprise Bird, Eagle or Rémire, Marie-Louise and Plate and vary from 66ac (26ha) to 174ac (70ha) in area.

The sand cays are typical palm-studded islands of the tropics, but the elevated reefs are semi-desertic in appearance. Each of them has its own distinctive quality. Bird and Desnoeufs are ornithological wonders during the breeding season of the sooty tern. Denis has a striking light-house, visible over the tops of the palm trees. Eagle has an immense fringing reef, which is a conchologist's paradise. Marie-Louise, one of the prettiest, has a tricky and exciting landing. Poivre, Daros, Alphonse and Providence have impressive coconut groves. Plate and Coëtivy, the most isolated islands, are separate little worlds. St Pierre and Assumption, which have been quarried for guano, look forlorn and forbidding. Cosmoledo has a ring of attractive islands and islets. Astove, the perfect atoll, has a lovely, almost completely land-locked lagoon and the most beautiful butterflies of the Seychelles.

Life on the coral islands revolves around the settlements which usually consist of the manager's house and office, the stores, the water tanks, the copra dryer, a small gaol and a small chapel. On the outskirts of each settlement is the workers' 'camp' of wooden and thatched cottages, where the indentured labour from Mahé and the other granitic islands live during their island tours. A ubiquitous building on the islands is the boat shed, from which the graceful, flat-bottomed pirogues are swiftly launched as soon as the inter-island schooner is sighted.

The 'monarch' of each of these isolated islands is the Administrateur, or manager, who not only cares and looks after the islands for the (usually) absentee owners, but also acts as head-boatman, store-keeper, accountant, builder, postmaster, doctor and, on occasions, priest.

THE ISLANDS' NAMES

The names of the various islands of the Seychelles recall the early exploratory history of the Western Indian Ocean. Of the main granitic islands, Mahé bears the name of Mahé de Labour-donnais, the French East India Company governor; Praslin that of Gabriel de Choiseul, Duke of Praslin and French Minister of Marine, and Silhouette that of Etienne de Silhouette, a French Comptroller-General of Finances. Among the smaller granitic islands, several, such as La Digue, Curieuse, Ste Anne, Cerf and Marianne, have been named after the sailing ships of explorers or early settlers.

27

Many of the coral islands recall administrators or the eighteenth-century sailors who discovered or reconnoitred them. Denis bears the name of Denis de Tobriand, who took possession of the island in the name of the King of France, while in command of the flûte *L'Etoile* in 1777. The nearby Bird island, which is better known as the Ile aux Vaches in Seychelles, has been named after numerous sea-birds, especially sooty terns, which breed on it. Its French name has its origin in the 'vaches marines', sea cows or dugongs, which were once found on it.

The Plate and Coëtivy group, south of the Seychelles plateau, consists of two isolated islands. Plate owes its name to its topography. It is flat and is so low that it is difficult to locate during rough weather. It was discovered and named by the Lieutenant de Lampériaire, of the goélette *La Curieuse* in 1769. Coëtivy bears the name of the Chevalier de Coëtivy who sighted it on 3 July 1771 while in command of the flûte *Ile de France*.

Portuguese Influence

The Amirantes, which figured on early Portuguese charts as the Ilhas do Almirante, or the Admiral's islands, are believed to have been named after Vasco da Gama who is reported to have sighted them in 1502 during his second voyage in the Indian Ocean. They comprise the African Banks, Eagle island or Rémire, Daros, Poivre, Boudeuse, Etoile, Marie-Louise, Desnoeufs and Desroches. The origin of the name of the African Banks, or *Bancs Africains* as they are better known in the Seychelles, is not known. They were discovered and named *Ilots Africains* in 1792, by the French Admiral Willaumez, who commanded the frigate *La Régénérée*. Eagle island, which is better known as *Rémire* in the Seychelles, bears the name of the Eastindiaman which visited it in 1771. The origin of its French name is not known.

Daros bears the name of the Baron d'Arros, Marine Commandant at the Ile de France from 1770 to 1771. Poivre bears the name of Pierre Poivre, the famous 'Peter Pepper' and Intendant of the Ile de France and Bourbon from 1769 to 1772. It was visited by the Chevalier du Roslan but was named by the

Chevalier de la Biollière in 1771. Boudeuse and Etoile are believed to have been named after the two ships of Bougainville's voyage round the world from 1766 to 1769. Marie-Louise was visited and named by the Chevalier du Roslan in 1771. It was the fourth island to be located by him during his voyage to the Amirantes, but the origin of its name is not known. Desnoeufs, or Desnoeuf, which means 'one of the nine', is believed to owe its name to the fact that it is one of the nine main islands of the Amirantes. It was, however, only the fifth island of the Amirantes located in 1771 by the Chevalier du Roslan who named it Ile des Neufs. According to E. de Froberville, the island's name should be des Noeuds. Desroches island, which is close to the Amirantes banks proper, was named after the Chevalier Desroches, the governor of the Ile de France and Bourbon from 1767 to 1772. It was explored by the Chevalier de la Biollière in 1771.

Alphonse, St François and Bijoutier make up the Alphonse group. Alphonse bears the name of its discoverer, the Chevalier Alphonse de Pontevez of the frigate *Le Lys*, who visited it on 28 January 1730. St François, discovered on the same occasion, was presumably named after the religious feast of St François de Sales on 29 January. The origin of the name of the third island of the group, Bijoutier, is not known.

St Pierre, Providence and Farquhar constitute the Providence group. St Pierre bears the name of the ship of Captain Duchemin who visited the island on 16 June 1732. Providence was named La Providence by the crew of the French frigate *L'Heureuse*, wrecked on a neighbouring bank in 1769. The Farquhar islands were formerly called Juan de Nova (or Jean de Nove), after Joao da Nova, the Galician navigator. They were renamed in 1824 after the first British governor of Mauritius, Sir Robert Townsend Farquhar. The islands were visited by the Chevalier de Pontevez in 1730.

In addition to Aldabra itself, the Aldabra group comprises Cosmoledo, Astove and Assumption. Cosmoledo atoll, according to d'Avezac, bears the name of an unknown Portuguese navigator, while the two main islands of the atoll, Menai and Wizard, were named after the ships of Captain Moresby who visited the atoll in 1822. Cosmoledo was sighted by Captain Nicolas Morphey of the frigate *Le Cerf* on 13 August 1756. The name of Astove, according to d'Avezac, is derived from the Portuguese words *as doze ilhas*, meaning the twelve islands, which he claims was originally the name of the Farquhar islands, but which was transferred in error to Astove. Astove was visited by Captain Lazare Picault of the tartane *L'Elisabeth* and Captain Jean Grossin of the boat *Le Charles* in 1742, on their way to the Seychelles.

Assumption island, which is better known by its French name of *Assomption* in Seychelles, was discovered by Captain Nicolas Morphey on 14 August 1756 and named after the religious feast of the following day. The origin of the name of Aldabra is uncertain. It has been said to derive from the Arabic 'al-Kadhra', meaning 'the green', and also from 'aldaraba', a type of door knocker of the same shape as the atoll. According to d'Avezac the atoll should be named 'Ilha da Area', meaning Sand Island, although this seems hardly appropriate. It has also been claimed that Aldabra could have been derived from the Arabic 'Al-Dabaran', which means the five stars in Taurus, more particularly the brightest of the group. If the first of these derivations is accepted, it could be attributed to the fact that the large lagoon of Aldabra produces a green reflection in the sky above the atoll which can be seen for miles out at sea. Aldabra was sighted by Captain Lazare Picault and Captain Jean Grossin in 1742.

GOVERNMENT

Under the latest Seychelles constitution, which came into force in 1970, the colony is administered by a governor and commander-in-chief appointed by the British Queen and he is assisted by a deputy-governor. According to the constitution the governor must consult the Council of Ministers in the formulation of policy and in the exercise of his powers. But he has direct control over external affairs, defence, internal security, the official press and radio and the public service. He also has an over-riding discretionary power and may act against the advice of the Cabinet of Ministers, if he thinks it right to do so. The régime of restricted democracy which exists in the Seychelles may be defined as 'government by consent'.

The Cabinet of Ministers is presided over by the governor and consists of three ex-officio members, the deputy-governor, the Attorney General and the Financial Secretary, the Chief Minister and four other ministers, the Minister of Agriculture and Natural Resources, the Minister of Housing, Labour and Social Services, the Minister of Aviation, Communications and Works and a Minister without portfolio.

The legislature or Legislative Assembly consists of a nominated Speaker, the three ex-officio members of the Cabinet of Ministers and fifteen elected members. The official language of the assembly is English but members may also speak in French.

There are twenty Government departments. The most important are the Secretariat, the Treasury and the Agricultural, Education, Medical, Civil Aviation, Public Works and Police departments. The heads of these departments are usually Seychellois. The majority of the professional officers, however, are still British expatriates. Rural administration is practically non-existent in the Seychelles, the whole territory being administered centrally from Victoria.

2   NATURAL HISTORY

THE islands have not a large flora, but a high proportion of it is endemic and therefore unique. Of the 500 or more plant species which have been recorded in the Seychelles, some eighty grow nowhere else in the world. The 'stars' among these botanical treasurers are the six Seychelles palms; the great broad-leaf forest hardwoods; two screwpines; two orchids; the curious pitcher plant, which is one of nature's marvels, and the jelly-fish plant which is the rarest and the most distinct of the whole of the Seychelles plants.

Similarly, among the 3,000 or more species of land animals found in the Seychelles, over eighty per cent of which are insects, a high proportion is endemic and unique. More than fifty per cent of the species of the insects recorded in the Seychelles belong only to this area. The proportion of endemism is even higher among the molluscs, amphibians, reptiles, birds and mammals. Some of the members of this unique fauna are very interesting. Among the crustaceans there is the small black Alluaud's crab which has been found up to 2,000ft above sea level. The insects include two small, rare cockroaches, four species of stick insects, the handsome and rare *Cirrhocrista*, *Thalassodes* and *Nyctemera* moths and the giant tenebrionid beetle of Frégate island. The more than sixty species of molluscs of the relict forests include two large, primitive acavid snails, one of which is found exclusively in the coco-de-mer reserves of Praslin island. In the freshwater streams of Mahé, Praslin and Silhouette is found the small but prettily spotted Seychelles killer-fish. Among the amphibians are the primitive, legless and dull coloured caecilians and five species of frog one of which, the large jade green *Megaxilus*, is a joy

32

to the eye. The reptiles include the only two Seychelles snakes, especially the delicately tinted *Boaedon* grass snake, and the small, pretty tiger chameleon. The indigenous land birds include six species which are among the rarest in the world, while the mammals are represented by a large, orange-breasted flying fox, and two small, very rare bats which were the only mammals to be found on the islands before man arrived there.

Three types of flora and fauna can be distinguished in the Seychelles. That of the sand cays, which consist of few species, is of little interest and consists mainly of plants and insects with a wide pan-tropical range, but some of these islands have large seasonal populations of sea-birds and are then ornithological wonders. For example Desnoeufs island, of the Amirantes group, which although only 86ac (34·4ha) in area is the home of some five million terns, especially sooty terns, from May to October each year during the breeding season in the Western Indian Ocean.

The flora and fauna of the uplifted reefs of Astove, Assumption, Cosmoledo and Aldabra, of the Aldabra group, are more interesting, being extensions of the fascinating flora and fauna of the neighbouring large island of Madagascar. Aldabra is one of the last virgin islands of the world whose flora and fauna constitute an almost untouched eco-system. Aldabra is the home of thousands of giant tortoises whose ancestors must have come from Madagascar, and of birds which are nearly all related to Madagascan species. Astove, Assumption and Cosmoledo, which are smaller and have been worked for guano, are less interesting.

The fauna and the flora of the granitic islands are much richer in species and are of great interest. Unlike those of the uplifted reefs, they have affinities in ascending order with the flora and fauna of East Africa, Madagascar and the Far East. From the bio-geographical point of view, the granitic islands of the Seychelles appear to constitute a western limit of the distant Oriental region rather than the eastern limit of the neighbouring Ethiopian region.

The first navigators to land in the Seychelles in the seventeenth and eighteenth centuries have left vivid accounts of the beauty of the forests which covered the islands, from the sea level to the top of the highest mountains, and of the large number of colourful birds and large crocodiles and tortoises which abounded.

THE PLANTS

There were three main forests. The lowland forest extended from the sea level to about 1,000ft. It was in this forest that the largest trees of the Seychelles were found. They were magnificent trees, over a hundred feet in height, up to fifteen feet in circumference and with fifty to seventy feet of straight trunk to the lowest branches. The tallest tree of this forest was the 'bois de fer'; a specimen of which was found to measure 190ft. It is the tallest recorded tree of the Seychelles. From 1,000ft to some 1,800ft extended the intermediate forest in which the trees were smaller than those of the lowland one. They formed a canopy at some sixty feet. The intermediate forest was the richest in endemic species of trees, shrubs and herbs, and, botanically speaking, was the most interesting. In it, on exposed boulders, occurred an interesting fern and orchid association. From 1,800ft upward occurred the mountain moss forest. This community was situated in the mist belt. Its trees were smaller than those of the lowland and intermediate forests, since they formed canopy at only forty feet. It is in this community that the remarkable pitcher plant of the Seychelles grew. There were also other plant communities at lesser altitudes and in drier conditions in north and south Mahé and in south-east Silhouette. On Praslin and Curieuse, there was the famous coco-de-mer palm. In another community, which occurred at about 2,000ft, on shallow and rocky soils, in central Mahé, was found the most distinctive plant of the Seychelles: *Medusagyne* or the jelly-fish plant.

After two hundred years of settlement, what is there left of this unique vegetation? The ancient forests in which large-leaf hardwoods, palms and pandani competed in beauty and robustness are no more, having been felled to provide timber for export

Page 35 (*left*) Pierre Poivre, famous French administrator of Mauritius and originator of the first French Settlement of the Seychelles, from an anonymous portrait—see page 28; (*right*) Quéau de Quinssy, the last and best known of the French administrators of the Seychelles, from an anonymous portrait

Page 36 Navigational aids: (*left*) one of the several inter-island coasters approaches Port Victoria. A buoy can be seen ahead on the left;

(*right*) the lighthouse, Denis Island, built in 1910

and for the early settlers' homes and their sailing ships. Further fellings of the re-generated forests were also made at the beginning of this century to supply fuel to the scented cinnamon leaf oil distilleries which were then springing up. In their place are now coconut groves and a medley of naturalised exotic small trees consisting mainly of cinnamon, cashew and coco-plum. There remain relicts of indigenous forests on the summits of Mahé and Silhouette, but they give but a pale picture of the original sylva.

Among the species which have survived, the most striking and interesting are palms, including the fabulous coco-de-mer palm, pandani or 'vacoas', among which are the handsome 'vacoa parasol' and the strange 'vacoa marron', some orchids, the pitcher plant and the jelly-fish plant.

The Seychelles are the home of no less than six endemic mono-typic and therefore unique species of palms. Their uniqueness indicates a very ancient history and they may be precious relicts from very early times when a predominantly palm flora would have been the characteristic vegetation of a large land area that may have existed in the Indian Ocean. They include the noble 'palmiste' palm which has been dedicated to the Baron von der Decken, a famous German explorer of Africa, and whose apical bud constitutes the true 'palmiste' of the millionnaire's salad; the splendid 'latanier latte' palm, which has been dedicated to the Belgian botanist Ambroise Verschaffelt and which has unusually broad, deep-green, undivided leaves and spectacularly prominent stilt roots; the pretty 'latanier hauban' palm, which has been dedicated to Albrecht Roscher, a young traveller killed in Nyasa-land, and which grows only on the summits of Mahé, Praslin and Silhouette, and the most famous of the palms, the coco-de-mer.

The Coco-de-Mer

To botanists the world over, the Seychelles are above all the home of that strangest of all palms, whose enormous, oddly-shaped nuts haunted the imagination of early navigators of the Indian Ocean and gave rise to fabulous tales. Coco-de-mer occurred originally on only five granitic islands of the Seychelles. Nowadays it is found growing spontaneously only on Praslin and Curieuse, having disappeared from the three neighbouring islets of Round, Chauve-Souris and St Pierre. This very curious distribution is very difficult to explain. It may have been a sequel to the dislocation and part disappearance in geological times of the large land mass of which the present granitic islands of the Seychelles are believed to be vestiges. During this time a large number of plant species must have disappeared, while others, like the coco-de-mer, became confined to islands and islets. In the case of coco-de-mer this isolation was final, since its nuts, when fresh and capable of germination, are heavier than water and cannot be dispersed by marine currents. On Praslin, where coco-de-mer is most numerous, there are three natural reserves of this palm, those of Fond Ferdinand, Anse Marie-Louise and Vallée de Mai. The latter, with its 4,000 coco-de-mer palms, is one of the botanical wonders of the world. Elsewhere on Praslin and on Curieuse there are only small clumps of coco-de-mer. The coco-de-mer palms to be found on Mahé and the other granitic islands as well as in botanical gardens all over the world have all been planted from nuts from Praslin or Curieuse.

It was only after the Portuguese had rounded the Cape of Good Hope and had penetrated to the Indian Ocean that the coco-de-mer nut became known in Europe. Before that it had only been known to the inhabitants of the Maldives, India and even Java, who sometimes picked on their shores strange, half-empty nuts which had been brought there by the sea. These nuts, shaped most strikingly like a female human pelvis, were coco-de-mer nuts from Praslin and Curieuse, which through decomposition of their hard, ivory-like endosperm had become lighter than water and had floated away. Because of their shape, their mysterious origin and also their rarity, these nuts captured the imagination of those who found them. They were believed to be the produce of a large submarine tree, hence the name of coco-de-mer or sea-coconut, and all sorts of virtues and properties were attributed to them : the partly disintegrated endosperm of the nuts was believed to have aphrodisiac properties while their shells were believed to be a sovereign antidote. Any such nuts were therefore worth a small fortune. It is reported that in the Maldives only the kings of these islands had the right to possess the nuts and that ordinary persons retaining them could have their hands cut off or even be put to death. Through early European explorers of the Indian Ocean, coco-de-mer nuts were introduced into Europe where they also became coveted possessions and were often used as drinking vessels, being heavily ornamented with gold and silver. The story is told of how Rudolph II of the Hapsburgs towards the end of his reign offered in vain 4,000 gold florins for a coco-de-mer nut which was then in Belgium and belonged to the heirs of the Dutch Admiral Wolfert Hermanssen who obtained it as a reward from the Sultan of Bantam, in 1602, when he delivered the Sultan's capital from the besieging Portuguese.

The first mention of the coco-de-mer in European literature is to be found in Pigafetta's account of Magellan's first voyage around the world, in which he gives a highly imaginary description of the coco-de-mer tree and of the place in which it was believed to grow. The coco-de-mer is also mentioned by the great Portuguese poet Camoens in his *Lusiads* in which he describes it as the antidote to the poisoner's malice. It is to the naturalist and sub-commissioner of marine of the King of France, Pierre Sonnerat, that we owe the first description of the coco-de-mer; it appeared in his now famous book *Voyage à La Nouvelle Guinée* published in Paris in 1776. The most famous description of the coco-de-mer entitled *Eden and its Two Sacramental Trees* is undoubtedly that of General Charles Gordon, which is still manuscript, in which the General, who visited the Seychelles in 1881, depicts these islands as the Garden of Eden and the coco-de-mer as the Tree of Knowledge.

It was only in 1768, more than 25 years after the first exploration of the Seychelles by the French, that the coco-de-mer was discovered on Praslin. It was found by a French surveyor, named Barré, who was working on the island and who did not believe his eyes when he saw the strange nuts. On seeing the first one near the shore, he buried it, planning to collect it later on. As he penetrated further into the interior of the island, he saw more and more nuts and could not believe that they could be the precious coco-de-mer. He nevertheless collected thirty nuts, which he took to Pierre Poivre, the famous Intendant of the French colonies beyond the Cape of Good Hope, in Mauritius. Poivre, who was a keen plant collector, was delighted with Barré's discovery and asked the Abbé Alexis Rochon, the French astronomer and geographer who was to visit the Seychelles the next year, to determine the exact locations of the islands and to bring back to him young coco-de-mer seedlings, which the Abbé did. Soon after its discovery, the coco-de-mer lost forever its reputation as a panacea and with it its fabulous value.

What does this curious palm, which is as famous as the Lebanon Cedar or the Giant Sequoia of California, look like? It is a dioecious, tall, extremely straight palm, whose clean, pillar-like trunk reaches up to 100 feet, whose large, rigid, fan-shaped leaves have a span of twenty feet. Its growth is very slow, since it takes nearly a millennium to reach its full size, and its strangely shaped nuts or seeds, contained in enormous, heart-shaped fruits, take seven years to mature. Weighing between thirty and forty pounds they are the heaviest and biggest seeds known.

Screwpines

'Vacoas' (pandani or screwpines) are tropical, palm-like shrubs or small trees, belonging to the family *Pandanaceae*. They are remarkable for their stilt-like aerial roots and for the handsome spiral arrangements of their leaves. They are popular as ornamental plants in botanical gardens and parks. There are six species of vacoas in the Seychelles, two of which, the 'vacoa parasol' and the 'vacoa marron', are among the more spectacular members of the islands' flora.

The 'vacoa parasol', which has been dedicated to John Horne, a former curator of the famous botanical garden of Pample-mousses in Mauritius, is a large tree, reaching some sixty feet high, with a smooth stem and high, umbrella-shaped branches with long drooping leaves and large multiple fruits with reddish-orange drupes. Very fine stands of this remarkable species are to be found near to or in the unique coco-de-mer reserve of the Vallée de Mai, on Praslin island.

The other outstanding screwpine of the Seychelles, the 'vacoa marron', reaches only forty feet in height, but has long aerial roots. It often grows on rocky outcrops and sends its roots, which may be 100ft long, deep down in ravines and river beds.

Leaf-Base Fauna

The Seychelles palms and screwpines have been compared with the plants of the family *Bromeliaceae* (to which the pineapple belongs) of the great tropical forests in which permanent marshes do not occur because of the intensive loss of water through transpiration and the drainage of the soil by roots. They constitute a habitat which has been likened to multiple, minute, aerial marshes, split up into numerous small pools at varying heights above the ground. Indeed, the Seychelles palms and screwpines, like tropical bromeliads, can store water and vegetable detritus in the axillary spaces between the bases of their leaves. This storage may subsist even during droughts, since the water is replenished by dew condensation during the night. This comparison is even more striking in the Seychelles mountain forests, where the great steepness of the ground affords little level space for any water to collect. These split, many-storied, diminutive ponds, containing fine humus and usually clear water above, harbour a fascinating fauna of their own. Among them are two small and rare pandanus-haunting cockroaches, with extraordinarily flat bodies which enable them to penetrate even the narrowest space between the screwpine leaves.

Orchid Species

Among the dozen species of Seychelles orchids are two striking ones. The commonest and the most beautiful is the 'fleur paille-en-queue', whose racemes of handsome, pearly white and pale green flowers have a delicious gardenia-like perfume, especially

41

at night. The local name for this plant is due to a long spur which gives its flower a vague resemblance to a tropical bird. It is the bridal flower of the Seychelles. This species is also found in Madagascar and the Comoros. It is usually found growing on boulders on the higher hills of Mahé, Praslin and Silhouette.

The other striking orchid is a vanilla, accordingly known as 'la vanille sauvage'. It is a leafless climbing plant which grows on bushes and rocks, especially on the latter, which it covers with a maze of serpentine growth. It is quite common on Mahé and Silhouette where it can be seen from sea level to the higher slopes. It produces large, attractive white flowers, with a flush of salmon pink inside. It is an endemic species and is not found outside the Seychelles.

Pitcher Plant

The most striking indigenous plant of the Seychelles is the 'liane pot-à-eau', or pitcher plant. There are some seventy species of pitcher plants in the world. All but two are oriental, and they range from Ceylon to north-east Australia. The two exceptions are a Madagascan species and the Seychelles one. The distribution of these plants is of special interest to geomorphologists, since it can only be explained in terms of Gondwanaland and continental drifts. All pitcher plants belong to the family *Nepenthaceae* which contains only the genus *Nepenthes*. This word, which comes from Greek words meaning 'without grief', was given by Linnaeus, the celebrated Swedish botanist, in an allusion to an episode of Homer's *Odyssey* and to the magical drug which Helen of Troy gave to Telemachus and Menelaus.

The Seychelles' pitcher plant was dedicated to a French gardener, naturalist and traveller, Auguste Pervillé, who visited the Seychelles in 1841 and who was probably the first person to collect it. Like other species, this one is a climbing plant with long narrow leaves whose mid-ribs are either prolonged as tendrils or terminate in striking, hollow, pitcher-like receptacles, complete with covers. It is because of these—they usually contain water— that the Seychelles plant owns its vernacular name. These receptacles are, in fact, insect traps for pitcher plants feed on insects attracted by the sugary secretions of the inner walls of the pitchers. A species of mosquito breeds in the pitchers.

The Seychelles pitcher plant is found in certain mountain recesses of Mahé and Silhouette in places with strong up-currents of cool moist air. It lives in close and only association with another endemic plant which acts as its support, the 'manglier de grand bois', which belongs to the family *Rubiaceae*, and which is reputed to bear the most beautiful indigenous flower of the Seychelles.

Jelly-Fish Plant

The most distinct of the plants of the Seychelles is *Medusagyne* or the jelly-fish plant. It is a small tree with spreading lateral branches, oblong coriaceous leaves, panicles of small rose-red flowers and fruits with winged seeds which when open look like jelly fishes. *Medusagyne* is also considered by some botanists to be a primitive flowering plant related to the camellias. Its unique quality meant that a new family of plants, that of *Medusagynaceae*, had to be created to contain it. This 'living fossil' occurs only on certain rocky outcrops of Mahé. From 1908 to 1970 it was believed extinct, but it has been rediscovered.

THE LAND ANIMALS

Birds

Of the 17 species of indigenous land birds recorded in the Seychelles, only two, a green parakeet and Marianne Island's White-Eye, have disappeared. The rest have survived the onslaught of man and that of his domestic animals and the exotic species which followed in his trail. Several of the remaining species, however, constitute minute populations which occur only on small isolated islands and islets, or in ecological niches on the larger islands, and are on the verge of extinction.

Among the commoner and less threatened species is a sun-bird, erroneously called 'colibri' in Seychelles; a broad-billed bulbul or 'merle'; a small kestrel or 'katiti', which feeds mostly on lizards, and the magnificent blue, or fruit, pigeon, which is dark blue, white and red and owes its local name of 'pigeon hollandais' to the fact that it had, before the event of the French tricolour, the same colours as the Dutch flag.

The rare species comprise the Seychelles bare-legged scops owl, or 'scieur', which occurs only on Mahé and is so named because its call resembles the noise of the pit saw; the Mahé white-eye or 'oiseau banane'; the Praslin black parrot, or 'cateau noire', which is to be found only in the vicinity of the Vallée de Mai; the magpie robin, or 'pie chanteuse', of Frégate island; the paradise fly catcher or 'veuve' of La Digue island, with long streaming black tail feathers; the foddy or 'toc toc' of Cousin, Cousine and Frégate; the red-headed turtle dove or 'tourterelle rouge', of which only a few specimens occur on Cousin and Frégate, and the brush warbler or 'petit merle des îles' of Cousin. These birds have acquired the rather sad distinction of being among the rarest of the world.

Among the exotic species are the ubiquitous Indian mynah or 'martin'; the crimson cardinal bird of Madagascar, or 'tisserin'; the oriental barred turtle dove, or 'tourterelle coco', and the Madagascan turtle dove, or 'tourterelle des îles'.

Crocodile Extinction

The crocodile found in the Seychelles which the settlers misnamed 'caïman' was the Nile crocodile. According to early visitors they were of enormous size, abounded on the islands and were even met at sea between the islands. They had terrible battles with sharks, and the noise could be heard for miles around during calm weather. The largest crocodiles are reported to have been found on Praslin and Silhouette. The largest to be found was shot on La Digue island, by Charles Oger in 1771. It was thirteen feet long and had a girth of eight feet.

Crocodiles became extinct in the Seychelles towards the middle of the last century, and live only in the accounts left by the early visitors. One of them, Louis Garneray, one of Surcouf's lieutenants, who visited the Seychelles in 1802, has told how he saw a negro capture a crocodile by first offering himself to it as a live bait. Théophile Frappaz, a French naval officer who called at the Seychelles in 1819, described how a settler seized a large crocodile which had attacked him and held it bodily until he was delivered by his blacks. Caïman river and bridge at Anse Boileau on Mahé, and Anse Caïman on La Digue recall that crocodiles once existed in the Seychelles.

Giant Tortoise

Extinction almost overtook the giant tortoises of the Seychelles, which reach up to five feet in length, weigh as much as 500lb and are the extraordinary survivors of a now vanished world. During the Tertiary Period giant tortoises occupied a vast territory in America, Europe and Asia, from which they disappeared about a million years ago except on certain islands between the Equator and the Tropic of Capricorn, where they abounded up to 200 years ago; the Galapagos in the Pacific Ocean and the Mascarenes; the Comoros; the Seychelles and Aldabra in the Indian Ocean. They are now found only in small numbers at the Galapagos and have disappeared from the islands of the Indian Ocean, except at Aldabra and the Seychelles.

At Aldabra, which is almost the last refuge of the giant tortoise, there are still thousands of these reptiles which wander over the immense coral ring of the atoll searching for food and water. There are also a few left in the Seychelles. They do not live in the wild state, however, being enclosed in back-yard pens in which they spend a semi-domestic life. At the beginning of the rainy season baby tortoises, the size of a match box, emerge from the soft spongy soil in which they are hatched. Some of these small tortoises, hatched when a daughter is born to their owners, will be kept to be sacrificed some 20 years later and served at the wedding feast of the now adult girl.

The most famous of the Seychelles tortoises is probably the one which the Chevalier Marion Dufresne brought to the Ile de France in 1768. It had the distinction of being handed over to the British in 1810, when the island, henceforth to be called Mauritius, was conquered by them. It was at least 200 years old when it died accidentally in 1918. It is now preserved in the British Museum, in London.

Chameleon

Among the other smaller but nevertheless striking examples of the land fauna of the Seychelles are a chameleon, caecilians and two insects, the leaf insect and the giant tenebrionid beetle of Frégate island.

There are some eight-five species of chameleons in the world. One is found in Spain and Palestine, another in India and Ceylon, a third in Seychelles and two in Arabia. The rest are found in Africa and Madagascar, especially in Madagascar, where there are thirty-five species. The largest chameleon, which is two feet long, and the smallest, which is only $1\frac{1}{2}$in long, occur in Madagascar.

The Seychelles' species, or tiger chameleon, is six inches long, greyish green in colour, with dark spots. It is a timid, harmless little animal and is still found at La Misère, on Mahé, and the Vallée de Mai in Praslin. A technophobe, it shuns human beings and is certain to become rarer as more land is cleared and its forested habitat recedes.

Caecilians

Caecilians, or apoda, are primitive, worm-like legless batracians and are known as 'vers de terre' in Seychelles, although they have only the appearance of earthworms. Dull in appearance, scarcely seen because of their burrowing and nocturnal habits, caecilians are nevertheless among the more interesting animals of the Seychelles. Although they look like small snakes they have no scales. Instead they have numerous circular grooves around their body. They have a short tail of the same thickness as their body. They can neither see nor hear although they can detect vibrations in the ground. Their eyes are covered with bone and skin, and they have no eardrums or middle ear structure. They have, however, two curious, feeler-like tentacles which can be extended at will from small pits between their nostrils and their eyes, on both sides of their head. They are used to taste food.

Caecilians are found in tropical regions of America, Asia and Africa where they live a hidden life in moist soil, generally near swamps, and where the females lay heaps of gelatinous eggs, which they guard by coiling around them. The embryos have feathery external gills which they shed when they hatch out, and can be observed through the transparent shell of the eggs. Unlike other amphibians such as frogs and toads, caecilians spend their aquatic stage not in pools or streams, but in the closed world of their eggs.

Rare elsewhere in the world, caecilians are quite common, sometimes even abundant, in the Seychelles, especially on La Digue and Frégate. There are one hundred species of caecilians in the world. The Seychelles has no less than six of these, all endemic to the islands and which tend to range as distinct, insular sub-species, each island having its own.

Leaf Insect

The most striking of the insects of the Seychelles is undoubtedly the leaf insect, or 'mouche feuille'. It is one of the world's most perfect examples of mimicry and well deserves its appellation of 'comedian of nature'. Not only does the main part of its large flat body closely resemble the leaf of the plants on which it lives and feeds, but its legs are also like leaflets and its head is like a small, green unopened bud. Its green colour, which is of the same tinge as that of its host plant, is sometimes speckled with reddish spots or streaks, resembling most realistically the rusty spots of diseased or ageing leaves. Another curious character of the leaf insect is its sexual dimorphism, the females being practically wingless while the male is capable of flight.

Leaf insects used to be common in the lowland forest of the granitic islands. Due to the almost complete destruction of their habitat they have now become rare. Four species of leaf insects have been recorded in the Seychelles. They are not endemic to

47

the islands, but range over the large oriental region, from the Seychelles to the Fiji islands. Their occurrence in the isolated Seychelles is another piece of circumstantial evidence pointing towards past land connections.

Giant Tenebrionid Beetle

Another very curious insect of the Seychelles is the giant tenebrionid beetle of Frégate island. It is most striking because of its size, shape and distribution.

Tenebrionids are usually tiny beetles fractions of an inch long. Frégate's giant tenebrionid beetle, which is over one inch long, is therefore the true giant of the family. More curious still is its shape. With its short, thick, round body and its long thin legs, it looks to the uninformed like a spider. It has no wings and bears on its back numerous small tubercles. Its appearance is so incongruous that when it was first described scientifically the writer was believed to have reported on a fictitious insect made up of parts of other beetles.

Its distribution is even more singular. It has been recorded in only two places in the world: the small Round island near Mauritius, and Frégate island in the Seychelles. It can still be found on Frégate, but is now extinct on Round island, where only one specimen was collected in 1869 at a time when the species was probably dying out there.

THE MARINE ANIMALS

If, apart from crocodiles and tortoises, there were originally no large animals on the Seychelles, there were, and still are, a considerable number of large game fishes in neighbouring waters. The 'vaches de mer', or dugongs, which provided the basis of the mermaid legend and which have given their name to two islands of the granitic group (Ile aux Vaches, or Bird, and Ile aux Vaches Marines), have been exterminated, and the number of green turtle and the hawksbill turtle has been greatly reduced. But there are still many dolphins, porpoises, giant rays, marlins, sail fishes and sharks, including the stupendous whale-shark, around the islands.

The most beautiful and spectacular fish of these waters are undoubtedly the blue marlin, the sail fish and the whale-shark.

Blue Marlin

The blue marlin, which is known as 'espadron' in the Seychelles, is the tropical version of the swordfish of temperate waters. It is a strong and fast fish, which may reach fifteen feet in length and weigh over 1,000lb. It is carnivorous and feeds on fishes and squids which it captures by running them through with its spear-like beak. The power and precision with which it attacks its prey makes the blue marlin dangerous to light craft on the high seas, since it believes any floating object to be a prey and attacks it. The blue marlin may even attack the fisherman who has captured it and overturn his boat.

Sail Fish

Still more sought after for its sporting qualities is the sail fish, or 'diable la voile', of the Seychelles. Closely related to the marlins, this fish has an enlarged dorsal fin which looks like a small sail when it is swimming near the surface. It is even claimed in the Seychelles that the fish can use its 'sail' to travel. The largest sail fish ever seen in the Seychelles was observed near Silhouette island in 1928. It measured some twenty-five feet long, being larger than the boat from which it was observed, and must have weighed about 1,500lb. When hooked, the sail fish has the habit of leaping into the air and 'tail walking' on the surface of the sea.

Whale-Shark

The whale-shark, better known as 'chagrin' in the Seychelles, is the largest fish in the seas. As its name implies, it is a shark the shape and size of a whale. It can measure up to sixty-five feet and can weigh over fifteen tons. Although so big, the whale-shark is harmless and feeds on plankton and other small marine animals which it engulfs in mouthfuls. Yet in the Seychelles the whale-shark is generally feared by fishermen, who accuse it of being malicious and of being especially fond of upsetting and even overturning fishing boats. This reputation is due to the fact that the whale-shark likes to rub against floating objects so that it can scrape parasites from its back. A whale-shark which surfaced under a small pirogue off Silhouette, in 1928, carried the boat and its two occupants for about half a mile before diving.

The Smaller Animals

The warm tropical waters around the Seychelles contain a large variety of fish and a rich invertebrate life, ranging from the tiny madrepores of the coral reefs to giant clams and from the wedge clams of the coral sand beaches to the octopus. The most beautiful fish are those of the coral reef, while the tastiest are the 'bourgeois' or red snapper and the 'bécune', which is a type of barracuda. The ugliest is the stone fish or 'laffe', which with the geography cone is one of the only two venomous creatures of the Seychelles.

The giant clams, or 'bénitiers', owe their French name to the fact that they are sometimes used as holy water stoops in churches. The shell of the largest clam known is reported to be in the St Sulpice church in Paris and to have been offered to the French King Francis I by the Republic of Venice. Giant clams are the largest shelled molluscs known, measuring up to four feet long and weighing as much as a quarter of a ton.

The wedge clams or 'tecs tecs' are tiny, delicate shells which burrow in the beaches. They make an excellent soup. The octopus, or 'ourite', is speared in the coastal lagoons and is another Seychelles delicacy.

Particularly beautiful among the intensive life of the shallow lagoons are the collectors' delights: the highly-polished cowries and olives and the variegated cones.

3   PRE-EUROPEAN HISTORY

THE first Europeans to land in the Seychelles in the seventeenth and eighteenth centuries found the islands uninhabited and with no signs of ever having been settled. Had man never set foot on these islands? Although situated in the middle of the Western Indian Ocean and therefore a long way from the peripheral routes adopted by the early navigators, it would have been strange if the Seychelles, however small and isolated, had not been visited at some time through the centuries.

Among the early navigators of the Indian Ocean were the Egyptians who as early as 2900 BC are reported to have established connections with the mysterious land of Punt, somewhere along the eastern coast of Africa; the Phoenicians who in 945 BC went in quest of the fabulous Ophir on behalf of King Solomon; the Romans who during the last century before Christ had established two quite separate routes in the Indian Ocean, one to the south, towards the land of Punt, and the other to the east; the Indonesians who towards the beginning of the Christian era are believed to have migrated to Madagascar, and the Arabs who from the seventh to the ninth centuries settled on the East African coast. It was the Indonesians and the Arabs, however, who are believed to have come across the Seychelles.

INDONESIANS

Indonesians, Polynesians or Indo-Malayans are known to have migrated and settled in Madagascar in several successive waves just before or at the beginning of the present era. They con-

51

stituted the Merina tribe. Their place of origin, migratory routes and the reasons for their migration are not known.

Did the Indonesians come directly from their original home or did they use staging points on the way? Opinions differ on this. At least one author, H. A. Lindsay, claims that this was so and also that the Seychelles were one of their staging points. According to this theory, the people in question originated around the Bay of Bengal and followed two migratory routes, one to the south-west and the other to the south-east to the islands off the coast of Sumatra, and that the voyages to the south-west ceased when canoes returning from the south-east brought the news that uninhabited, fertile islands had been found. It would have been during their voyages to the south-west that the Indonesians used the Maldives and the Seychelles as staging points before finally reaching Madagascar. This theory, which does not appear to be borne out by any archaeological evidence, also holds that it was the migrants to the south-west who finally peopled the broad stretches of the Pacific Ocean.

A rather tenuous piece of circumstantial evidence in support of this staging-point theory was the presence in the Seychelles and Madagascar of the Indo-Malayan casuarina tree which the first European explorers found growing on these islands, but which was absent from the Mascarenes and the other islands in the Western Indian Ocean. In the Seychelles it was common enough for a place, Anse aux Pins, on the East Coast of Mahé, to be called after it. Since casuarina seeds do not float and should not therefore have been dispersed by marine currents, it was inferred that the casuarina tree had been introduced by Indonesian migrants, both in Seychelles and Madagascar. One author, Jonathan D. Sauer, claims, however, that casuarina seeds could have been rafted in their cones or in crevices in logs or pumice stone and may have reached the Seychelles and Madagascar in this way. This opinion is based on the fact that seedlings of casuarina germinating on stranded pumice stone have been found on Krakatoa beaches. It does not account for the fact that casuarina occurred only in

Page 53 Sail and steam: (above) MS *Lindblad Explorer*, a tourist vessel built in Finland and registered in Norway, seen from the Aldabra atoll; (below) local trading ketch moored in Port Victoria harbour

Page 54 (above) Visitors approach La Digue island in typical landing launch; (below) one of the trucks or 'camions' for touring Mahé island. The narrow coastal road is typical

the Seychelles and Madagascar, of all the islands of the Western Indian Ocean, before the arrival of the Europeans.

It appears more plausible that the Arabs knew about the Seychelles and may have visited them. Early Arab travellers in the Indian Ocean included Al-mas'udi who is reported to have visited Madagascar in 916, and Ibn Battuta, the greatest of the Muslim travellers of the Middle Ages who journeyed up the East African Coast and visited the Maldives in the fourteenth century, so reaching the vicinity of the Seychelles.

The Arabs who settled on the East African coast between the seventh and ninth centuries to escape religious or political persecution must have known about the Seychelles. A vessel of one of them, Hassan ibn Ali, who is believed to have been the son of a sultan in Shiraz, is known to have travelled to the island of Johanna in the Comoros in 975. From the African coast and the Comoros the Arab colonists also reached Madagascar and the three Mascarene islands of Mauritius, Reunion and Rodriguez, which they named Dina Margabin, Dina Moraze and Dina Arobi. They did not settle in the Mascarenes but had settlements in Madagascar. The Comoros were completely dominated by the Islamic influence. It would have been strange if while crisscrossing the sea around the Seychelles the Arabs never came across these islands.

Moreover, although the ancient monsoon routes which the Arabs took, and still take today, to sail to and from the East African coast from the Persian Gulf lie north and west of the Seychelles, they must sometimes have strayed or been blown off course and may then have encountered the Seychelles.

The only archaeological evidence of the presence of Arabs in the Seychelles appears to be some thirty tombs which existed near the shore at Anse Lascars, on Silhouette, and which are believed to have been those of the crew of a wrecked dhow.

These tombs, which were to be seen until 1910, have now been washed away by the sea.

It has also been claimed that the Arabs, who are known to have introduced the coconut palm to the East African coast, may also have done so in the Seychelles, since the first European explorers of the islands found rows of this palm growing along the beaches. But coconuts are easily dispersed by the sea and could have reached the Seychelles by water. However, as found by Thor Heyerdahl during his famous Kon-Tiki expedition, coconuts immersed in sea water soon loose their germinating power. The nuts kept in baskets on the deck of the Kon-Tiki remained edible and capable of germination all the way to Polynesia, while those which were kept below deck and were washed by the waves were ruined. On the other hand, after careful experiments, C. H. Edmonson has estimated that coconuts retain their viability up to 110 days after floating in the sea and can thus be dispersed over a distance of some 3,000 miles (4,800km).

After an exhausting survey of the evidence on the origin of the coconut, E. Chiovenda came to the conclusion that the coconut palm evolved into its present form through natural selection on coral islands in the Western Indian Ocean. On sifting all this evidence, one could conclude that the coconut palm reached the Seychelles by natural means. One would then also expect it to have been present on all the islands of the colony. Yet while coconut palms were seen growing on Mahé and the other granitic islands by the first European explorers, there was none on the two small coral islands of Bird and Denis which are situated on the northern edge of the Seychelles plateau and are only a relatively short distance away.

That the Arabs did not settle in the Mascarenes and the Seychelles can be attributed to the fact that these islands were deserted and that, apart from the coco-de-mer palm on Praslin and Curieuse which they must have missed altogether, had nothing to attract them.

4   DISCOVERY AND SETTLINGS

THE earliest name of the Seychelles, that of *Sete Irmanas* or the Seven Sisters, is believed to have been given to the islands by the Portuguese during their early voyages in the Indian Ocean. There is no record of their having ever landed in the Seychelles. They were probably too busy plying from the East African coast to the riches of India to do so. Furthermore they were so well equipped for long voyages that they did not have to stop on isolated islands. They must, however, have sighted the Seychelles on the way, especially when they started to make occasional short cuts and avoid the longer route along the East African coast which took them as far north as Malindi before they sailed across the Indian Ocean. Joao da Nova is reported to have discovered the Farquhar islands in 1501 and Vasco da Gama to have sighted and named the Amirantes in 1502, while the first known map to show the Seychelles, that which the Portuguese cartographer Alberto Cantino made for the Duke of Ferrara, is dated 1501.

The first recorded landings on the Seychelles were made over a century later in 1609 by an expedition of the English East India Company under the command of Alexander Sharpeigh. This is known as the Fourth Voyage of the East India Company. The expedition came across the Seychelles while it was on its way to establish trade connections in Aden and Surat. It consisted of three vessels, the *Union* and the *Ascension*, which had been fitted out in England and set sail from Woolwich in March 1608, and the *Good Hope*, a pinnace which was built at the Cape of Good Hope. The *Union* became separated from the two other vessels during a storm and did not visit the Seychelles, but went on to

Sumatra after a landing in Madagascar where the captain and five men were killed by natives who attempted to seize the ship. Accounts of the voyage are contained in the journal of John Jourdain, an employee of the company. This journal remained forgotten for 300 years until it was published by the Hakluyt Society in 1905. The unnamed islands mentioned in the journal were then identified as the Seychelles by Rcar-Admiral Sir William Warton who had carried out hydrographical surveys in Seychelles waters. The expedition reached the Seychelles on 19 January 1609 and spent ten days there, during which landings were made on North Island and Mahé. The crews of the two vessels were delighted with the islands, which were uninhabited but abounded in water, fish, fowl and fruits. After leaving the Seychelles, the expedition's ships were the first British ones to sail the Red Sea. It returned to England in 1617.

Historical Accounts

The account left by Jourdain, the first to have been written on the Seychelles, gives a valuable picture of what the islands looked like in their primeval beauty. Jourdain's account is as follows :

Jan 19—About nine in the mornings wee descryed heigh land, which bare of us East and by South. At three in the afternoone wee sawe other ilands, which wee made to bee four ilands, and in the eveninge they bare of us north and by east some five leagues of. And wee stoode with a slacke saile all night untill towards the morninge, and then we stoode in for the land to seeke water and other refreshinge. At noone per observation 4d. 20m.

Jan 20—In the morninge, beeinge neere the land, wee slacked our saile and tooke our skiffe to goe sowndinge before the shipp, and to seeke a good place to anker in. Soe they came to a small iland [North Island] beeing nearest unto us, which lyeth about twoe leagues to the north of the heigh iland [Silhouette] where they landed in a faire sandy cove, where wee might have ankored very well, but because our men made no signe of any water we ankored not. Soe the boate retourned

58

and brought soe many land tortells as they could well carrie. Soe wee stoode alonge towards the other ilands. The tortells were good meate, as good as fresh beefe, but after two or three meals our men would not eate them, because they did looke soe uglie before they weare boyled; and soe greate that eight of them did almost lade our skiffe. Goinge alonge by the ilands wee found 10 and 12 fathome within a league of the ilands, and 2 leagues of wee had 20 and 30 fathome faire shoaldinge. This evening wee thought to have ankored at an iland which laye E.N.E. of us, which seemed to be a very fruitful place and likelye of water; but beinge neare night, and perceyveinge some shoalds and rocks neere the land, and other ilands ahead of us, wee brought our tacks aboard and stoode to the offinge N.E. and by North, hopinge the next daie to finde good ankoringe at the other ilands which wee saw further to the E.N.E. of us [Praslin etc]. But in our course there was a small iland [Mamelle] which laye about 2 leagues of the shoare, which we would not double but weare faine to goe betwixt the ilands and it, haveinge faire shoaldinge 15 and 20 fathome. This small iland is noe other than a rock, alias ilheo. And being passed this rock, wee stoode upon a tacke until midnight and then with a slacke saile wee stoode for the eastermost ilands with a fresh gale. Wee stoode West and by North and W.N.W. for soe wee had brought the body of the ilands of us; haveinge seene this daie above 30 ilands, little and greate, faire shoaldinge round about them. I mean to the northward of them. The distance from the southermost of these ilands to the norther of those wee saw maye bee neare 20 leagues, close by one another.

Jan 21—In the morninge wee stoode in for the land, sending the skiffe before the shipp to sound, as alsoe to finde a good place to anker in. Soe aboute nine in the forenoone wee came to anker in 15 fathome water, within halfe a mile of the land. But wee found it full of small rocks, wherefore wee wayed and went further in, where we found cleare grownd and better rideinge; where wee found very good water in dyvers places, but noe signe of any people that had ever been there—[Sir Wm Wharton concluded that their final anchorage was under St Anne Island]. It is a very good roade betwixt two ilands aboute a mile and a halfe distant from iland to iland; and there lyeth, betwixt the E.S.E. and S.E. and by East other 3 ilands [Cerf, Long and Moyenne] aboute 3 leagues of the place where wee ankored, soe that wee weare in a manner land locked, except towards the E.N.E. and E. To know the place where wee ankored, there is a small iland [Mamelle] which lyeth next hand north from the road aboute 2 leagues and there is a rock or ilheo [The Brisans] lyinge betweene the iland where wee ride and the foresaid iland, the roade beinge to the south-wards of that. To the W.N.W. there is a very high iland some 10 leagues of which was the first iland wee descryed [Silhouette]. Wee ankored in 12 fathome water. The road is in 4d. 10m. to the southward.

Jan 22—Finding a rowlinge to sea to come in out of the E.N.E., wee warped in about two cables length farther and ankored in 13 fathome water, very good ground and within a pistoll shott of the shoare; where wee ride as in a pond from the 22th to the 30th ditto, in which time wee watred and wooded at our pleasure with much ease; where wee found many coker nutts, both ripe and green of all sorts, and much fishe and fowle and tortells (but our men would not eate any of them, but the tortells we could kill with staves at our pleasure) and manye scates with other fishe. As alsoe aboute the rivers there are many allagartes [el legarto—alligator], our men fishinge for scates tooke one of them and drewe him aland alive with a rope fastened within his gills. On one of these ilands, within 2 miles where wee roade, there is as goode tymber as ever I sawe of length and bignes, and a very firme tymber. You shall have many trees of 60 and 70 feete without sprigge, except at the top, very bigge and straight as an arrowe. It is a very good refreshing place for wood, water, coker nutts, fish and fowle, without any feare or danger, except the allagartes; for you cannot discern that ever any people had been there before us.

French Expeditions

Strangely enough these enthusiastic accounts did not incite the company to annex the islands. Except for the European pirates, who had been chased out of the West Indies to settle on Mada-gascar in the early eighteenth century and who are said to have used the Seychelles as temporary bases, the islands were not visited again for 133 years. The next visit was thus made by the French from the Ile de France, which is now Mauritius, during the first of a series of expeditions which led to the settlement of the islands.

Whereas the first landings of the English on the Seychelles were incidental, the French expeditions were planned and appear to have had two main motives : firstly the reconnaissance of the islands which lay in the direct sailing route to India and were potential navigational risks especially during the 'counter-monsoon', or north-east monsoon of India, and secondly the anxiety to forestall British occupation at a time when the French and the English were in acute competition to establish supremacy in the Indian Ocean.

The first two French expeditions were carried out by Lazare Picault in 1742 and 1744, on the order of Mahé de Labour-donnais, the French East India Company's governor of the Ile de France and Dourbon (now Mauritius and Reunion). Lazare Picault's first expedition consisted of two ships, the tartane *Elisabeth*, which was under his own command, and another small vessel, the *Le Charles* under the command of Captain Jean Grossin. The first landing was made on 22 November 1742, at a small bay in the south-west of Mahé which has been known since then as 'Baie Lazare'. The expedition left four days later, after loading thirty-three giant tortoises and six hundred coconuts. On leaving, Picault named Mahé 'l'Ile d'Abondance'. Unsatisfied with this hasty exploration (Picault is reported to have made a navigational error of three hundred leagues) Labourdonnais sent him back two years later, in 1744, with a qualified draughtsman to chart the islands. Picault, again on the *Elisabeth*, reached Frégate island on 28 May, moved to a point close to the present Port Victoria on 30 May, left for Praslin, which he named 'l'Isle de Palme', on 10 June and left the islands on his way back on 14 June, after naming them 'Iles de Labourdonnais' and renaming the 'Ile d'Abondance' as Mahé, all in honour of Mahé de Labourdonnais. Picault's enthusiastic descriptions of the islands, which he reported to be covered with tortoises and crocodiles and to abound with birds, recall those of John Jourdain more than a century previously.

That Picault's expeditions were not followed by an occupation of the islands may be attributed to the War of the Austrian

Succession which had broken out in Europe, but in which the French and English East India Companies became involved in India. Mahé de Labourdonnais led an expedition on the Coromandel Coast which resulted in the defeat of British naval forces under Peyton and the capture of Madras, and so he had his hands full. Furthermore, on his return to Mauritius in 1746, he found that he was in disgrace and had been replaced as governor-general.

Twelve years passed before the next French expedition to the Seychelles. This took place in 1756 and was ordered by Governor-General Magon. It had as its main object the formal possession of the islands, which it was rumoured the English wanted to occupy, in the name of the king of France and of the French East India Company. It was led by a young and promising officer, Corneille Nicolas Morphey, and also consisted of two vessels, the frigate *Le Cerf* under the command of Morphey and which was to give its name to Cerf island, near Port Victoria, and the goélette *St Benoît* under the command of the Sieur Préjean. Morphey was of Irish origin.

The expedition reached Mahé on 6 September. After thoroughly exploring Mahé Morphey took possession of the islands at sunrise on 1 November in an impressive ceremony, at which the Royal Standard of France was broken from a high flag mast. There was a salute of nine guns from the ships and three cheers of 'Vive le Roi' by the shore party. An already prepared stone (which French ships carried for establishing the right of possession on uninhabited islands), bearing the fleur-de-lis surrounded by the Cordon du Saint Esprit and surmounted by the crown of Louis XV, was set up on a fan-shaped rock facing the harbour. A formal act of possession was drawn up and signed by Morphey and the officers present. By it Morphey took possession of Mahé and of seven other islands to the east, which he named 'Seychelles' in honour of the Vicomte Moreau des Séchelles, the then Comptroller General of Finances of France.

Morphey's descriptions of Mahé tell of thick mangrove groves along the east coast, of crocodiles, ten to fourteen feet long, which were numerous and which could even be seen up to the mountain tops where they destroyed the especially large tortoises found there, of large carp and trout in the streams, of coastal fringes of coconut palms and of large lowland trees, fifteen to sixteen feet in circumference and seventy-five to eighty feet in height. He concluded that no permanent advantage could be obtained from a settlement on the islands because of their mountainous nature, but praised the port where two hundred vessels could ride in safety and be beached and careened. Morphey was apparently unable to visit Praslin because he was short of provisions, but is reported to have named that island 'Ile Moras', in honour of a French minister of that time. Morphey also drew a map of the port, which is a model one for that time.

That Morphey's expedition was not followed by an occupation of the islands may be attributed to the Seven Years War which was to cost France her Canadian possessions.

Twelve years passed before the launching of the next French expedition, that of the Chevalier Marion Dufresne. He had been a captain of the by then defunct French East India Company and had experienced a varied and colourful career at sea. It was he who in 1746 brought back to France Prince Charles-Edward, the young Pretender, after his defeat at Culloden. He was massacred by natives in New Zealand in 1772 during an exploratory voyage undertaken from Mauritius, and died in circumstances curiously similar to those of James Cook's death in Hawaii six years later. The Seychelles expedition, which lasted from December 1768 to January 1769, consisted again of two ships, the flûte *La Digue* and the goélette *La Curieuse*, which had been fitted out by Desroches, the Governor of Mauritius, and the Intendant, Pierre Poivre. Mauritius, which the French Government had just 'bought back' from the bankrupt French East India Company, was then administered under a new system by a governor whose powers were confined to naval, military and political affairs and an intendant who had sole powers over finance, justice, public works and agriculture.

The first administrators under the new system were Governor Daniel Jean Dumas and Intendant Pierre Poivre, who assumed duty in 1767. Dumas was succeeded by Desroches in 1768. Unlike the preceding ones, the Dufresne expedition appears to have been more than an exploratory one for Dufresne is reported to have been granted the two ships so that he could exploit the islands' timber. The commercial aspect of the voyage appears to be substantiated by the fact that the Lieutenant de Lampériaire, who was in command of the *La Curieuse*, was allocated a detachment of a corporal and four men to work the forests of Praslin and by the many references in Dufresne's journal to the commercial prospects of the islands' tortoises, turtles and fish.

During the visit, La Digue and Curieuse islands were named after the ships of the expedition and l'Ile Moras was renamed Praslin, in honour of the then French Minister of Marine, Gabriel de Choiseul, Duke of Praslin and cousin and collaborator of Etienne François, Duke of Choiseul-Ambroise, Louis XV's famous minister. A stone of possession bearing the arms of France was also set up in a small bay in the north of Praslin, which has been known since then as Anse Possession. It was during this expedition that the surveyor Barré found the coco-de-mer palm growing on Praslin, an important botanical discovery. Dufresne reported that Praslin was covered with dense, impenetrable forest and uninhabitable but considered Mahé more favourably because of its abundance of coconut palms, tortoises, turtles and fish. He also reported its harbour to be excellent. Dufresne's expedition had an unfortunate sequel. One year later, in September 1769, the Sieur Duchemin, who had been the second in command of the *La Digue* and who knew of Barré's discovery, sailed to Praslin on the palle *L'Heureuse Marie* which he loaded with coco-de-mer nuts and dumped on the Indian market, thus destroying for ever the fabulous price of these nuts.

Bad-tempered Navigator

There was one more French expedition from Mauritius before the settlement of the islands. It took place in 1769 and again consisted of two vessels, the corvettes *L'Heure du Berger* and *Le Vert Galant*. The leader of the expedition and captain of the first vessel was the Chevalier Grenier, while Lieutenant de Lafontaine commanded the second, smaller vessel. With the expedition was a French savant, the Abbé Alexis Rochon. No cleric, although he had the title of Abbé (he had never been ordained and was married), Rochon was a brilliant hydrographer and astronomer who was engaged before the advent of the chronometer in finding an easy and practical way of determining longitude at sea by calculating the distances between the moon and the sun. He was also bad tempered and pettishly obstinate, which resulted in his often being on bad terms and at cross purpose with the masters of the vessels on which he was travelling.

The object of Rochon's visit to the Seychelles was to observe during the voyage the transit of Venus and to determine the exact position of the islands. Rochon was prevented from making his astronomical observations, as on the day of the transit of Venus he was within 'an inch of being shipwrecked' off the Cargados Carajos islands. This incident gave him the opportunity to vent his temper on D'Après de Mannevilette, the famous French hydrographer and author of the monumental set of nautical charts known as the Neptune Oriental, whom he accused of incompetence. He reached the Seychelles safely, however, and spent one month there from 13 June to 14 July. On Mahé and the neighbouring islands he found monstrous crocodiles and on Praslin, which he called l'Isle de Palme, he collected coco-de-mer seedlings for Poivre in Mauritius. Rochon River, on the bank of which he camped, and Rochon Dam, both on the island of Mahé, recall the visit of the scientific Abbé.

To Rochon is also owed an original description of Barré's discovery of the coco-de-mer palm on Praslin. It reads :

He found on the Isle de Palme, on the edge of the shore, a fruit which he first took for a coco-de-mer nut. He hid it carefully, but having penetrated in the forest he saw regretfully that the ground was covered with these fruits and with the trees which produced them. These trees reach a height of fifty feet. Their head is crowned with ten to twelve fan-shaped palms of 20 feet in length; each of these large palms is born on

65

a six-foot stipe and this stipe is indented in its contour. From the axis of the leaves springs a ramified panicle whose branches end in female flowers; the pistil of the flowers gives, in maturing, a fruit which, with its husk, may weigh fifty pounds.

While examining carefully this forest, Barré persuaded himself that the nut of that island could not be the true coco-de-mer nut. He contented himself in collecting, out of curiosity, about 30 nuts which the famous Poivre formally declared to be this fruit so sought after in India and the whole of Asia; from then on he speeded up our departure in order to obtain quick information on this subject.

Further French Expeditions

The year after the Grenier expedition the Seychelles received its first settlers. There remained, however, another group of islands to the south-west of the Seychelles proper, the Amirantes, which was scarcely known and presented navigational risks. It was therefore important to reconnoitre them as well. These islands were visited in 1771 by two more expeditions from Mauritius: that of the Chevalier du Roslan in January 1771, and that of the Chevalier de la Biollière in November of the same year. The du Roslan expedition consisted of two vessels, the corvette *L'Heure du Berger* which had already visited the Seychelles in 1769, and the corvette *L'Etoile du Matin*. Du Roslan commanded the first vessel while the Chevalier d'Hercé commanded the second one. For the second expedition, de la Biollière had only one vessel, which was again the *L'Etoile du Matin*. The first expedition explored the southern islands of the group before proceeding to the Seychelles to find out how Brayer du Barré's settlement, which had been started in the preceding year, was getting on. The second expedition visited the Seychelles to land further settlers, livestock, provisions and seeds before exploring the northern islands of the group. These islands were taken possession of only much later, in 1802, by the Sieur Blin, of the goélette *La Rosalie* which had sailed from the Seychelles expressly for that purpose. During the first expedition an officer of the *L'Heure du Berger*, Lieutenant Charles Oger, took a formal possession of Silhouette and La Digue islands, on 28 January and 12 February respectively. Silhouette bears the name of Etienne de Silhouette, the French Comptroller General of Finances of 1759. This was the same Silhouette who gave a new word to the French and English languages : as he wanted to replenish the Government treasury his critics called drawings consisting only of outlines 'silhouettes' to symbolise the state to which his financial measures were reducing the tax-payers. No stones of possession were used on these occasions, but acts of possession were written and signed. That of La Digue was sealed in a bottle which was placed in a small stone pyramid on the island.

English Expeditions

To complete the account of the explorations of the Seychelles one must mention an English expedition which also took place in 1771. On hearing that the French had settled in the Seychelles in the preceding year, the British East India Company's Government of Bombay decided to explore the islands between the Maldives and Madagascar. Some of these islands, like the Chagos, were as yet uninhabited and it was feared that the French might occupy them. The expedition consisted of two Eastindiamen, the *Drake* and the *Eagle*. The vessels carried two surveyors of the Bombay Marine, Lieutenants Robinson and Thomas. The expedition visited the Seychelles, the Amirantes and the Egmont islands of the Chagos archipelago, during which Mahé's harbours, Bird island and Eagle island (of the Amirantes) were surveyed. A chart of Bird island was also prepared by a third officer of the expedition, Lieutenant Buncombe. It was during this expedition that Rémire island acquired its English name of Eagle. It was also probably during this expedition that the alleged burning took place of Curieuse island by the crew of the *Eagle*, which, it has been imputed, wanted to destroy the coco-de-mer palms of the island after taking a load of the precious nuts. This expedition was followed by several English surveys of the islands of the southwestern Indian Ocean which led to a short-lived English settlement on Diego Garcia, of the Chagos, in 1786.

5   SETTLEMENTS CREATED

IF the French explorations of the Seychelles from Mauritius were inspired by the need to reconnoitre islands which lay in the direct sailing route to India and by the fear of their eventual occupation by the English, the settlement of the islands appears to have been due mainly to Pierre Poivre's belief that because Mahé was on the same latitude as Amboyna and Banda, the spice islands of the Sunda Strait, they would be especially suitable for the growing of spice.

For many years Poivre had dreamed of establishing spice plantations in Mauritius to break the Dutch monopoly. Before he was appointed Commissaire-Ordonnateur of Mauritius in 1767 (he received his commission of Intendant in 1771) he made several attempts to obtain spice plants for the French East India Company. The few plants or seeds he obtained died or did not germinate. In 1770, however, he managed to obtain a large quantity of nutmeg seeds and seedlings and a small quantity of clove seedlings from Geby island, of the Moluccas. Most of these were dead by 1771, and Poivre began to think that Mauritius was not suitable for spices and that he ought to try to grow them on other islands in the Indian Ocean and in tropical America. A second expedition to the Moluccas was arranged and on its return, in June 1772, Poivre decided to distribute the seedlings which consisted of more cloves than nutmegs. They were sent to Reunion, the Seychelles and Cayenne. The seedlings for the Seychelles left on 1 July 1772.

The Seychelles had already been settled for some two years. The prime mover of this first settlement was Brayer du Barré, a colourful adventurer. He arrived in Mauritius in May 1770 after

68

being for three and a half years the official receiver of the Lotterie de l'Ecole Royale Militaire at Rouen, a post in which he is reported to have been particularly efficient. He quickly attracted the goodwill of Governor Desroches and of Pierre Poivre and with their support he began to build three ships, the *Duc de Praslin*, the *Thélémaque* and the *Comte de St Florentin* with the intention of joining in the slave trade. Like so many adventurers of his time he probably planned to make a quick fortune by privateering. However, even before the vessels were completed he thought of another project, that of a settlement in the Seychelles. He must have heard accounts of the islands from the members of the last two expeditions to visit them. One cannot help thinking that Pierre Poivre, who had been impressed by Brayer du Barré's spirit of enterprise, must have thought of him as a possible founder of his projected spice plantations on Mahé. Poivre had just received his first consignment of spice seeds and seedlings from Geby and must already have been thinking of sending some to Mahé.

By 12 August Brayer du Barré had obtained the necessary authorisation from Desroches and Poivre. The *Thélémaque* left the same day with the first settlers and with the help of a good south-east wind reached the Seychelles on 27 August. The conditions laid down by Desroches and Poivre were that the settlement was to be on Ste Anne Island, which is the largest of the ring of islands facing Port Victoria, and that it would be Brayer du Barré's responsibility to cut timber for the buildings, to fish, to provision his settlement at his own expense for nine months and to furnish all the implements necessary for the works as well as the arms and munitions which the settlers might need to defend themselves.

Captain's Report

The names of the first fifteen settlers who came from Reunion island were recorded in the official report of Captain Lécore, the master of the *Thélémaque*. They were Delaunay, the Commandant, Anselme, Berville, Drieux, Jean-Marie Fustel, Charles

Aumont, Joseph Bonneavoine, Jean Thomas, Gorineau, Louis Vervière, Claude Givant, La Rüe, Bernard, a surgeon, Lavigne, a master-carpenter and Jean-Jacques and Michel, two servants. In addition there were seven slaves, five malabaris and one black woman.

All appears to have gone well at first. News of the settlement was received from the Chevalier du Roslan of the *L'Heure du Berger* and the Chevalier d'Hercé of the *L'Etoile du Matin*, who visited the Seychelles in January 1771. They reported that the plantations were successful. This delighted Brayer du Barré. He wrote to the Duc de Praslin, who was then the French Minister for the Colonies, to report the successes :

> M. Delaunay [the Commandant] has had houses and stores built . . . Rice and maize are flourishing perfectly, as well as manioc and all kinds of vegetables. The seeds from the Ile de France, especially the coffee, have surpassed all expectations.

He also suggested another settlement on the main island of Mahé, on a plain behind the Stone of Possession and watered by three rivers. These first successes must be credited largely to Poivre who not only supplied Delaunay with planting material but also gave guidance on how to grow the produce.

Poivre, pleased with these results, authorised Brayer du Barré to start the new settlement, and sent him forty white and black workers, cows, poultry, seeds and provisions on de la Biollière's *L'Etoile du Matin* before this ship began its exploration of the Amirantes. On the corvette was also Antoine Nicolas Benoît Gillot, a retired officer of the regiment at Pondicherry and an ex-captain of the militia at the Ile de France, who had been given two missions, a private one from Brayer du Barré and an official one from Poivre. The private mission was apparently to choose the site for the new settlement. The official one was, of course, to find a suitable site for a spice plantation. The *L'Etoile du Matin* reached the Seychelles on 30 October 1771. Gillot was badly received by Delaunay, who when told by Gillot that assistance would be sent on the senau *La Marianne* replied that

Page 71 Landings by boat: (above) sheltered landing beach on the coral island Alphonse; (below) this tender from MS Lindblad Explorer has to make course through more turbulent water to reach Aldabra atoll

Page 72 Beaches: (*above*) Beau Vallon beach, Mahé, a popular place for bathing and relaxing; (*below*) seine netting also at Beau Vallon. Seine netting is used specially for catching small fish for use as bait

the settlers needed neither bread nor wine, but only blacks to work, and that they knew how to eat maize. After these rather strained beginnings, Gillot had difficulty in obtaining a boat and a crew to visit Mahé, but managed to do so from 1 November 1771 to 15 February 1772.

A Settlement Fails

The site of the new settlement was chosen near the mouth of the Rochon River on Mahé. The new settlers started to clear the land while Gillot surveyed Mahé looking for a site for the spice garden. Brayer du Barré's luck must have changed about then. The new settlement was a failure and its settlers had to be transferred to Ste Anne some three months later. There they replaced the first settlers who were then due back in Mauritius. With them on the senau *La Marianne* went Gillot, who reported to Poivre that he had found a suitable site for a spice garden on Mahé. From then on matters must have gone from bad to worse for Brayer du Barré for in 1773 La Pérouse, the famous French navigator, who on a voyage from Pondicherry put in at the Seychelles to shelter from bad weather, reported the Ste Anne settlement to be in a deplorable state with the men starving and destroying the tortoises and turtles instead of cultivating the land. The next blow came with the replacement of Desroches and Poivre, who had been Brayer du Barré's sponsors, by D'Azac de Tenay and Maillard Dumeslé in the administration of Mauritius. They not only refused to ratify the concession accorded to Brayer du Barré in 1770, but obtained a judgement against him in 1775, condemning him to pay the cost of equipment originally despatched on the *Thélémaque*.

Brayer du Barré was an indefatigable and skilled letter writer who wrote lengthily to various people at the Versailles Court, including the King whom he must have annoyed at times with his demands and recriminations. In a new spate of letters he appealed in vain to officials and friends in France, claiming that he had been misled by Poivre, cheated by Delaunay and Gillot and slandered. Unabashed by the obvious failure of his Ste Anne

E

settlement he was still brimming with plans for further settlements in the Seychelles. He wrote unsuccessfully to Loius XVI to ask for authorisation to set up establishments on Cerf Island, Silhouette and La Digue. Was he responsible for the rumour that a silver mine had been found on Ste Anne and did he thus hope to create interest in his settlement? In any event he was arrested for having invented the story and for having inveigled thirty or forty settlers of Mauritius to emigrate to Ste Anne. He was released in 1776, on the condition that he left Mauritius. He sailed for Pondicherry where he died in 1778. By 1773 all the Ste Anne settlers had been removed on the Chevalier Grenier's *La Belle Poule* at the order of de Ternay and Maillard Dumeslé. This ended the first attempt at settlement by Brayer du Barré who never set foot on the Seychelles himself.

Spice Planting

When the Ste Anne settlers had gone the Seychelles were not left uninhabited for Gillot had already started a settlement on Mahé at the end of 1772. This was at the request of Poivre, who was determined to grow spices on the island. Poivre must by then have had doubts about Brayer du Barré's settlements or was anxious to speed up the spice planting.

The site chosen by Gillot for the spice garden, which was to be called the Jardin du Roi, was at Anse Royale on the east coast of Mahé. This is how Gillot described it in a report which he submitted to Poivre when he returned to Mauritius on the *La Marianne* on 12 April 1772 :

> The part approximately to the south-south-east is the one which has been chosen for the Jardin du Roi; it may have one league or more in width and nearly one in depth. The soil there is black and deep, the bottom is sandy. It has a very large swamp which is passable everywhere and two fine rivers. At the back of this garden is a fine hill wide and gentle which leads to a small well wooded plateau which I believe to be more than two leagues in circuit whose soil is excellent and fairly well watered. This cove is named the Anse Royale and has in its reef a very fine

channel and a 'barachouas' sheltered from the north-west winds.

The Jardin du Roi is situated at the Anse Royale, it has a square surface of fifty gaulettes of fifteen feet each, this surface is divided into four square of twenty five gaulettes each, with in between a cross-shaped space of the thickness of two gaulettes of standing trees. Two of these squares will be cleared, with the reserve of soft-bark trees spaced at twenty feet; the two others will be cleared entirely. All the squares will be planted all round with a single row of banana trees, the first will be planted with banana trees spaced at fifteen feet and planted in quincunx, and the second in coconut palms at the same distance equally in quincunx, the third with 'nourouc' [Indian coral tree] or spiny wood also in quincunx and the fourth with only its row of banana trees all round. All this work will be done, as it is stated, for the months of June and July.

On leaving for Mauritius, Gillot instructed Delaunay to start preparing the site according to the plan drawn up by him. The *La Marianne* was wrecked on its arrival in Mauritius. Gillot was safe however and sailed back to the Seychelles on 1 July, on the corvette *Le Nécessaire* which was commanded by Jacques Cordé. He had been appointed director of the royal garden with a salary of 2,400 livres tournois per annum. He brought back the precious spice plants, nutmeg, pepper and cloves which Poivre had recently obtained from the Moluccas, and cinnamon from Ceylon, as well as some of the King's blacks to work the land. He is also reported to have been accompanied by his younger brother and by Pierre Hangard, an old soldier of the French East India Company, and a few of his slaves. Hangard is regarded as the first permanent settler of the islands, for he died on Mahé in or about 1807 after obtaining a concession. Gillot was also the bearer of precise instructions from Poivre to Delaunay about the assistance he was to be given. While the new settlement was to be totally independent from that of Brayer de Barré, it was nevertheless to receive help from it in the form of raw material, labour and services, such as the use of the blacksmith's workshop, but these were to be paid for. This arrangement led to an acrimonious claim from Brayer du Barré in 1773, which stated that Gillot had been supplied with 1,548 days' work and various effects.

Troubles and Recriminations

Gillot appears to have met with trouble from the start. First he did not get on with Delaunay, the former commandant of Ste Anne who had been replaced by Anselme some time in 1772, but who had stayed on to help Gillot. There were arguments and quarrels between them. There was also a deadlock between the two settlements. The King's 'blacks' revolted and ran away. Maroon slaves raided the garden. There were also quarrels with Brayer du Barré who was furious because Hangard, to whom he objected, had been appointed an overseer of the royal garden and had also temporarily occupied the settlement of Ste Anne when du Barré's settlers had been moved out. Eventually Gillot was stranded without food and had to exist on a diet of maize for 15 months. It is not surprising that the garden did not prosper. In 1775 when Gillot returned to Mauritius for a short period, during which the garden was taken care of by Hangard, there were only five nutmeg trees, four cinnamon trees, one clove tree and forty pepper plants in it. By then Poivre had left Mauritius and its new administrators, de Ternay and Maillard Dumeslé, had none of his interest in spice growing. They had even removed the King's 'blacks' from Gillot's responsibility. In a letter dated 24 July 1775 and addressed to de Sartine, the then French Ministry of Marine, Gillot complained bitterly of the treatment he had received and claimed that he had incurred a heavy financial loss of some nineteen thousand livres tournois while taking care of the garden. Gillot soon returned to the Seychelles however and resumed responsibility for the garden. In 1777 the administrators in Mauritius withdrew their support and the garden became the property of Gillot, to whom it was granted as a concession. Embittered and disillusioned, Gillot continued to look after the garden until its disappearance in May 1780.

So ended in failure what has been described as the second

attempt at the settlement of the Seychelles. It was not completely fruitless, however, since the cinnamon introduced in 1772 was eventually to become the second in importance of the crops of the Seychelles.

In 1778, however, there arrived at Mahé, on the royal corvette *L'Hélène,* the Lieutenant de Romainville. He was an 'ingénieur' and had taken part in Bougainville's famous voyage round the world from 1766 to 1769, at the end of which he had settled in Mauritius. De Romainville was the first military commandant of the Seychelles, and he was accompanied by fifteen soldiers. The new arrangement decided upon by la Brillane, the then Governor of Mauritius, had originally been suggested by de Ternay and Maillard Dumeslé, who had been dissatisfied with Brayer du Barré's and Gillot's settlements and who appear to have wanted the islands to be occupied by the military so that the English would not contest their French ownership. The military administration lasted until the end of the French occupation. The Seychelles remained a dependency of Mauritius, however, until 1903 when they became a separate British Crown Colony.

6   COLONIAL GOVERNMENTS

WITH the arrival, in 1778, of Lieutenant de Romainville, there was what many described as the first serious
attempt at the settlement of the Seychelles under a
competent administrator. Unfortunately, de Romainville's term
of office was not a long one for he fell ill and returned to Mauritius in 1780. He died there in 1781.

The primary need was for settlers. De Romainville took the first
step in this direction by granting concessions to Hangard,
Delaunay and Gillot who had decided to stay in the Seychelles.
With the help of his soldiers, who were paid 27 sols each per day
and were expected to fell timber for the repair of calling ships,
de Romainville also laid the foundation of what was to become
the Colony's administrative centre. This was called 'l'Etablissement du Roi' and was set on the only suitable site facing the
harbour which became known as the Port Royal.

De Romainville was, unfortunately, also responsible for the
destruction of what remained of the Jardin du Roi at the Anse
Royale. He had received precise instructions on leaving for the
Seychelles that the precious spice plants should be destroyed if
the Colony was threatened by an enemy. In May 1780, a ship
flying the English colours was seen approaching Mahé. As English
ships from India were known to be poaching coco-de-mer nuts
on Praslin and it was rumoured that the English intended to
start a settlement in the Seychelles, de Romainville gave the order
to set fire to the garden. The approaching ship was, in fact,
French.

De Romainville was succeeded in 1780 by Berthelot de la Coste

78

who proved to be a poor administrator and had to be recalled to Mauritius in 1783. He was replaced by Gillot until the arrival, in 1788, of Louis Jean Baptiste Philogène de Malavois.

Gillot continued de Romainville's work and granted small temporary concessions to retired officers who wanted to settle in the Seychelles. He had no authority to grant permanent concessions and as a result was at loggerheads with the settlers. In 1785 there were only seven settlers in the colony, occupying 120 arpents (125ac or 5ha) with 123 slaves. Among the settlers were the Chevalier d'Offay, a retired naval officer, and Savy, a retired army officer from India, who had recently arrived in the Seychelles with their families and slaves. Descendants of these two early settlers are to be found among the leading citizens in the Seychelles today.

Changing Policies

De Malavois was a former army officer of the French East India Company and an 'ingénieur-géographe'. He had already visited the Seychelles from 1786 to 1787 to carry out survey work. In him the budding Colony had one of its most conscientious, imaginative and capable administrators. De Malavois is reported to have been sent to the Seychelles by the Vicomte de Souillac and Motais de Narbonne, the new administrators of Mauritius, with detailed instructions calculated to crush any existing enterprise. No inhabitants were to take any tortoises, hawksbill turtles, coconuts or even wood without the permission of the commandant. All existing concessions were to be revised and bachelors were not eligible for any; no settler could sell his property without the authority of the administrators at Mauritius and anyone leaving the Colony without presenting a solvent successor was to forfeit his possessions. The object of these restrictions was obviously to make way for the new, planned concessions which de Malavois was to grant and also to attract keen and serious settlers instead of those only interested in exploiting the natural resources for quick profit.

De Malavois is especially remembered for his nine comprehensive memoirs of the Seychelles dating from 1787 to 1803; for the land concessions which were granted on his recommendation and which enabled the colony to grow out of its protracted embryonic stage by attracting new and competent settlers, and by his firmness which is still recalled in the Seychelles by the saying 'temps de Malavois', whereby hardly treated persons are apt to express their resentment. Judging by his memoranda on the islands' timber, tortoises and turtles, which contain recommendations on how they should be preserved, de Malavois must have been one of the earliest conservationists. De Malavois resigned in 1790 when he was succeeded by Caradec who, in turn, was succeeded in 1791 by Nageon. De Malavois is known to have stayed in the Seychelles until 1802.

In his memoirs de Malavois wrote about the geography, the soils, the land, the timber trees, the coconut palms, the tortoises and turtles, the state of the King's buildings and of the harbour and the means to defend it. He considered the harbour to be especially suitable as a port of call for vessels plying between Mauritius and India and for dealing in the slave trade on the East African coast, as well as a staging or rallying point for vessels intended for action in India, or as a retreating base in case of French set-backs in India or Mauritius. Among the memoirs, the most interesting are perhaps those which describe the trees, of which he lists fourteen types, and the tortoises and turtles. The following account of how the hawksbill turtle, or 'caret', was and to a large extent is still captured in the Seychelles reads :

Besides, here is the way in which this fishing is carried out here, whose season starts towards the end of August and lasts until that of December. The caret, as is known, is a species of turtle which like the one about which we have spoken, comes to lay its eggs on sandy shores; during the 4 months of the fishing, the caret lays twice. It always choses for climbing on the shore the time of the half-rising tide; it is then that the black workers turn it and open it; the complete eggs are removed from it and buried in the sand and, when they succeed, take 50 days to hatch. The plastron, which is of no use, is removed as well as the hind legs and the entrails; the remaining meat, of which one is careful not to use because it upsets those who eat it, is allowed to rot.

At last, at the end of a few days, the actual shell loosens from the bones of the caret in each of which are found 13 sheets, both large and small, namely : 6 large ones on the sides and 7 on the back. There is moreover a kind of indentation in detached parts at the bottom and all round the shell which furnishes several pieces of shells which are less prized; each caret produces generally $2\frac{1}{2}$ to 3lb of shell of all types.

There is one more way of fishing for carets; it is the same which is used for the green turtle. When a caret wishes to climb on the beach, it visits the reefs over which it must pass and from there observes whether it can deposit its eggs on the shore. Before it can get there, one or two blacks in a pirogue go and attack it with their 'vare' and dress it as has been just explained.

The model concession planned by de Malavois was to be of 108 'arpents' (112ac or 4·5ha) each and to consist of twenty-seven 'arpents' of forest reserve, ten of grassland, five of building space and the rest of land for growing crops. Of this, half was to be used to grow food-crops for the blacks and the other for growing rice and maize. He estimated that each concession would produce 22,800lb of paddy and 28,500lb of maize annually, from which 13,000lb of paddy and 20,000lb of maize would be available for sale. De Malavois also estimated that the thirty-six concessions, or 'habitations', which could be provided on Mahé should be able to produce an annual surplus of 250,000lb of rice and 30,000lb of maize for sale to the garrison and passing ships. This estimate was greatly exceeded in due course when the Colony assumed a ship victualler's rôle.

In September 1792 the Sieur Enouf, who had been appointed Civil Administrator of the Seychelles in the place of Commandant Nageon, arrived on the frigate *La Fidèle*. He was accompanied by Daniel Lescallier, one of the four commissioners who had recently been appointed by the French National Assembly to introduce the new constitution of revolutionary France in the French establishments beyond the Cape of Good Hope. The other three were Jacques-François le Boucher, Marc-Antoine Pierre Tirol and

Joseph Pierre Dumorier. Both Enouf and Lescallier were unable to land on Mahé, having been quarantined on Ste Anne island because of a fear of smallpox. The quarantine period over, Enouf went to Mahé where he took up the post of administrator. He instituted the universal suffrage, created a Colonial Assembly which, because of its smallness, was unable to send a delegate to Paris, and founded a National Guard whose members proudly bore on the buttons of their uniform the words 'Iles Séchelles'. Enouf, who appears to have been resented by the settlers probably because of his connection with Lescallier, failed to obtain their support. Some of them, it is reported, threatened to leave the Seychelles. This was the reason why Quéau de Quinssy was appointed to replace him in 1794.

Little or no harm came to the Seychelles during Enouf's term of office. Under his administration the islands entered an eventful period which lasted throughout the revolutionary years and the Napoleonic wars.

Following the New Order

The settlers did not wait until the arrival of Enouf and of the special envoy Lescallier to fall in line with the new order in France, whose early phase of constitutional monarchy must have been welcomed by them. Or as it appears from the following series of events: on 19 June 1790 all the inhabitants of the Seychelles (less the slaves, of course) unanimously decided to constitute themselves into a Permanent Colonial Assembly; on 15 November this Assembly elected a permanent administrative committee of five members, which was also invested with municipal powers; on 16 December the Assembly invested itself with the criminal as well as civil judiciary power, under the authority of the King and the sanction of his representative; on 23 December, in a decision which aimed at severing the ties with Mauritius, the Assembly declared its independence from any other colony and on 17 July of the following year the Assembly elected a Juge de Paix and appointed a Board of Conciliation to consider appeals against his judgements.

The colonists took their new functions seriously, a fact which is further demonstrated by the formality with which they acted on special occasions, such as at the reception for the Civil Commissioners Gautier and Yvon, whom David Charpentier de Cossigny, the Governor-General of Mauritius and Reunion, had instructed to call at the Seychelles to tell the colonists about the principles of the revolution. It appears from the report to Charpentier de Cossigny that the Commissioners were unable to change the constitution which the citizens of the Seychelles had already granted to themselves. But in a letter to the Commandant-General they stated:

> It is with the greatest pleasure and in all fairness that we wish to testify to the interest which this infant Colony deserves. Perfect peace and order are established there and the mode of organisation which has been adopted does not appear to be of any major inconvenience, while it is in relation with the small size of the population and with the impossibility of constituting itself without diverting slightly from the present principles.

The Chevalier Jean-Baptiste Quéau de Quinssy (who later spelled his name 'Quincy') was the last French commandant of the Seychelles. He stayed in the islands after they had been ceded to Britain and died in Mahé at the age of 79 in 1827. He was buried in the grounds of Government House. De Quincy street in Victoria and the De Quincy village at Pointe Conan on Mahé have been named after him.

THE ENGLISH DEMAND SURRENDER

De Quinssy's administration is especially remembered for the Colony's capitulations to the British navy, the arrival of the French Jacobin terrorists and the neutralisation of the small merchant fleet of the Colony. Soon after his arrival on 16 May 1794 de Quinssy was faced with his first major crisis. Five warships under the French flag were seen approaching Mahé and anchored off Ste Anne island. They were, in fact, an English squadron under the command of Commodore Newcome. The long expected and dreaded moment of invasion had at last arrived. The inhabitants were convened by gun shots, fired at four minute intervals, and assembled at l'Etablissement. An English lieutenant came ashore carrying demands from Commodore Newcome for the immediate delivery of food for the English crews and for diseased French prisoners on board the *Dugouay-Trouin*, which had recently been captured. The demands were verbal, a fact which appears to have upset de Quinssy. He refused them on the grounds that honour did not permit him to help his country's enemies. The English then issued a written ultimatum to him to surrender the Colony within one hour or to suffer the consequences. De Quinssy could not hope to oppose the 1,200 men and 162 guns of the British with his own small forces and an Act of Capitulation in seven articles, drawn up in French by de Quinssy and bearing Newcome's notes in English alongside each article, was signed at 9am the next day, 17 May, on board HMS *Orpheus*. This document shows de Quinssy's foresight and cleverness. The Act provides for the protection of the inhabitants, their slaves and property. The commandant, it states, was to be a prisoner of war during the stay of the British squadron. The brig *Olivette*, owned by the corsair Jean-François Hodoul who had retired in the Seychelles, was taken and an occupation force of thirty men under a lieutenant was landed at l'Etablissement. To the toll of drums, a discharge of muskets and slow fire from the guns of the battery the French flag was lowered. Amid gunfire from the vessels in port, the English flag was hoisted. The British vessels, however, also continued to fly the French colours. A French vessel, *Les Deux Andrés*, passing near Mahé saw what she believed to be French vessels in the harbour and came in. When she discovered her mistake she tried to back out but had to surrender after receiving a broadside from HMS *Resistance*. On board this vessel were 400 slaves intended for Mauritius. They were taken to India instead.

In the morning of 31 May, two weeks after the arrival of the English squadron, the thirty men who had been put ashore were re-embarked and next morning the British vessels sailed away, leaving behind forty sick Frenchmen and 200 French prisoners-of-war who had escaped from the British ships on rafts and had remained hidden in the forests of Ste Anne and Mahé. These men, who could not be maintained in the Seychelles because of the precarious food situation, were sent to Mauritius.

Second Capitulation

As soon as the British vessels were out of sight, de Quinssy hoisted the French flag. He repeated this act after the second capitulation made to Captain John Wood of HMS *Concord* in 1804 in almost exactly the same terms as the first, and he did so on five more occasions. The capitulations were ratified each time by visiting British warships which were imposing a blockade on Mauritius, namely the *Sybille* and the *Victor* in August and September 1801, the *Terpsichore* and *Pitt* in August 1805 and the *Duncan* and the *Albion* in June and August 1806.

After the second capitulation, de Quinssy was reprimanded by General Decaen, the governor of Mauritius, for the readiness with which he had apparently given in. It seemed that de Quinssy had not waited for a formal order from the enemy to surrender the Colony. Decaen's instructions had been that he should make a show of resistance for honour's sake, but de Quinssy continued to ignore these instructions. He had good reasons for doing so for the object of the British raids was only to obtain water and to give the crews a chance to stretch their legs. On the one occasion that a token of resistance was made—on the arrival of HMS *Terpsichore* and the *Pitt*—de Quinssy hoisted the French flag and fired a shot. The result was that a party of twenty men and two officers landed and held him prisoner until the ships left that evening. Looking over the years one wonders what else de Quinssy could have done? That his action, in the circumstances, cut off as he was from Mauritius by very superior enemy forces, was the only sensible one is borne out by the respect which he won from the British navy and, with one exception, the consequent leniency which that navy showed towards the inhabitants of the Seychelles. The exception was HMS *Duncan*'s visit to the Seychelles on 7

November 1805. This frigate was in search of French privateers from Mauritius, which were then harrying British shipping in the Indian Ocean. Assisted by the brig *Emilie*, which she had previously captured and armed, she prowled around for the privateers. Near Thérèse island, the *Emilie* found the slaver *Courrier des Séchelles*, whose cargo of 170 slaves had been hidden on the island. Having failed to obtain the slaves, Captain Sneyd sent a party of 50 men ashore to pillage the settlements of the Sieurs Blin and Dupont, the owners of the *Courrier des Séchelles*. Before leaving five days later with the *Emilie* and the *Courrier des Séchelles*, this time without ratifying the previous capitulation, the *Duncan* also destroyed the goélette *La Rosalie* and the brig *Le Syrius*, which were suspected of being privateers.

Naval Battles

During de Quinssy's administration the Seychelles received the deported French Jacobins who had been accused of responsibility for the attempted assassination of Napoleon and Josephine by the *Machine Infernale* while they were driving to the Paris Opera on 24 December 1800. The seventy deportees were embarked at Nantes on the corvette *La Flèche* and the frigate *La Chiffone*. The *La Flèche* left on 15 February 1801 with thirty-eight deportees, and the *La Chiffone* on 13 April, with the remaining thirty-two. The *La Chiffone* reached the Seychelles first, on 17 July 1801. The *La Flèche* arrived only on 4 September. Both vessels, after their long and successful voyages, were to meet their fate in the Seychelles, in the course of the only two naval actions to have taken place in the Seychelles waters.

On her way to the Seychelles the *La Chiffone* was dismasted on 16 June in the Mozambique Channel while capturing the *La Bellone*, an Eastindiaman with a rich cargo from India. After despatching the captured vessel to Mauritius, she sailed to the Seychelles where she was stripped of her guns. She was being refitted when, on 20 August, HMS *Sybille*, of fifty guns, entered the harbour. After twenty-five minutes of combat *La Chiffone* was put out of action, with thirty-five dead and fifty wounded. To save the wounded and forty English prisoners from the *La Bellone* who were on board, the captain of the *La Chiffone*, Captain Guiyesse decided to surrender. During the battle the small vessel *Le Paracti Pacha*, a Portuguese prize of the privateer *La Nymphe*, which was in port, was also sunk, and two brigs from Mauritius, the *La Sophie* and the *Le Petit André*, were seized. A few days later HMS *Sybille* sailed with her prizes.

In a good old fashioned naval battle, the *La Flèche* put up a longer fight against HMS *Victor* which had been shadowing her for two days. The action took place on 5 September, the day after her arrival in the Seychelles. It lasted two and a half hours and left the French vessel with twelve dead and seventeen wounded. The *La Flèche* sank with her flag flying. It is reported that after the action Captain Collier of HMS *Victor* met Captain Bonamy of the *La Flèche* at the house of Commandant de Quinssy, and congratulated him on a gallant defence in what he described as one of the fiercest actions he had ever taken part in. He invited him to come aboard the *Victor*.

The Jacobin Deportees

The decision to deport what remained of the Jacobin terrorists of the French Revolution to the Seychelles was taken by Napoleon, as First Consul, after the attempt on his life in the Rue Saint-Nicaise, in Paris, while he was driving with Josephine to attend a performance of Haydn's oratorio *The Creation*. Napoleon appears to have believed at first that the attempt had been the work of the terrorists, since there had been four previous attempts on his life by them. When it was discovered that the last coup had been that of royalist insurgents he persisted in his decision to purge Paris and France of the last of the 'bloody terrorists'.

Among the seventy who were eventually deported to the Seychelles, the most sanguinary appear to have been Antoine Boniface, whose gods were Robespierre and Marat and whose wife is reported to have drunk the blood of victims of the September 1792 massacre; Louis Monneuse, who as a 'People's judge' presided over the killing of 171 persons, including the Princesse de

87

Lamballe, Queen Marie-Antoinette's friend; Jean Mamin, who is reputed to have cut open the breast of the unfortunate princess and to have pulled out her heart; Pépin Desgrouhette, a police informer, who at the St Lazare prison indicated to the Public Prosecutor those detainees whom he thought especially suited for the guillotine, and André Corchant who, with Parein, was responsible for the execution without trial of 1,684 inhabitants of Lyons.

Believing that the Government would never dare to deport them from France, or, if it did so, that they would soon be released by the assassination of Napoleon and the collapse of the Consulate régime, the deportees offered little or no resistance on the way and declined to take any effects or their families with them. They were never told where they were going and, as the voyage proceeded, were kept guessing all the time.

After crossing the Equator the *La Chiffone* (on her maiden voyage) started drifting towards the coast of Brazil and fought and defeated two Portuguese vessels. She eventually rounded the Cape of Good Hope and entered the Mozambique Channel in which she had another engagement, this time with an English vessel, the *Bellone* which she also captured and sent to Mauritius. On 11 July, after a voyage of eighty-nine days, she reached Mahé. Captain Guiyesse then disembarked with one of the deportees, Pierre Richon, who was very ill and who died soon after landing. It was only on 14 July, however, that the other deportees were allowed to land, after Captain Guiyesse had persuaded the Commandant of the Colony, Quéau de Quinssy, and the inhabitants to allow them to do so. The inhabitants consented to the deportees being landed only on Praslin, which was at that time uninhabited, but they finally agreed to their landing on Mahé provided they were kept at l'Etablissement in the custody of a detachment of soldiers who had sailed with them. On landing the deportees were addressed by the Commandant, who urged them to keep the law. They all replied that their conduct would be irreproachable. De Quinssy appears to have been touched by their destitution, for he told them that they would

Page 89 Houses: (above) thatched homes of coconut plantation workers on Desroches island; (below) planter's house on Silhouette island

Page 90 (above) Houses in the shade under Trois Frères Mountain; *(below)* view from beach house on Cousin island, near Praslin, at sunset

find in him a protector and a comforter and that he would write to France and request that their families be allowed to join them. They were then each issued with a jacket, five handkerchiefs, sweet potatoes, turtle meat, vegetables, fish, lard, salt and a little bread for the sick.

The deportees expected to join the first batch of thirty-eight who had left Nantes on the *La Flèche* almost two months before them. The *La Flèche*, which had not been seen at Mahé and which was therefore thought to have been sent to another destination or to have been lost on the way, arrived on 25 August after a dramatic voyage lasting more than six months.

Soon after leaving France she had been chased by two English vessels. She escaped them, but having broken her fore-mast had to put in for thirty-six days in a Spanish port, where one deportee attempted to escape but fell overboard and was nearly drowned. Another escaped but was recaptured. In another Spanish port, where the vessel put in for another month for more repairs, the deportees were told that Napoleon had been assassinated. Exhilarated by this false report, they demanded to be taken back to France and when they were refused they approached the Spanish authorities with no more success. On leaving harbour and having heard that the deportees were plotting to capture the ship Captain Bonamy had all of them locked up. Short of food, the *La Flèche* called at St Denis, of Reunion Island, to re-victual after 200 days of voyage. Leaving Reunion on 14 August, the vessel finally reached Mahé on the 25th of the same month. The deportees, who looked like skeletons, disembarked immediately, less Delrue who had died on the way.

What did the deportees think of the Seychelles, so far away from France and the agitated life they had led there? Not much, as appears from the following extract of a letter from one of them, Laporte, a previous public scribe, to his wife :

> Mahé Island is sinister; there are only 50 inhabitants. The 108 acres of land which have been allocated to the detainees are impossible to clear and are not worth 4 acres of good land of France.

F

The settlers were greatly concerned by the presence of the deportees on the island and, although they housed some of them in their homes so that they could keep a closer watch on them, protested to the authorities in Mauritius and even threatened to leave the Colony.

The first unpleasant incident occurred when three of the deportees, Louis-François Serpolet, Laurent-Derville and Magnian started to frequent a free negress by the name of Vola-Malaëfa and during a dance plotted to seize power. On hearing about this the Commandant, Quéau de Quinssy, convened a meeting of settlers and of some of the deportees. They decided unanimously that Serpolet and three negroes, Germain and Jolicoeur, who belonged to Vola-Malaëfa, and Fernando, who belonged to the Commandant himself, should be deported to Frégate until further notice. The order, which bore the signature of nine of the deportees, was duly executed.

When the news about the plot, accompanied by vehement letters of protest from the Mahé settlers, reached Mauritius the Colonial Assembly there decided that if any of the deportees attempted to land in Mauritius they would be put to death and also urged that all the deportees should be expelled from Mahé.

Most of the sixty-six deportees remaining on Mahé were more anxious than ever to leave the island on which the situation had become unbearable for both them and the settlers. The Commandant, as could be expected, was opposed to the deportees leaving the island. The situation appeared to have no solution, but the settlers attempted to find one. Apparently without the knowledge of the Commandant they agreed to assist the deportees to procure a boat to take them away. The project came to nothing, however, since before the completion of the boat there arrived in Mauritius, on 13 March 1802, the corvette *Le Bélier*, under the command of Captain Hulot, with the Capitaine d'Artillerie Lafitte on board. The latter, acting as Government Commissioner, had been ordered to arrest all the deportees and take them to Anjouan island, of the Comoros. This decision had been taken by General Magallon, Governor of Mauritius, and the Colonial Assembly of that island without reference to France.

After conferring with Captain Lafitte on board the *Le Bélier*, Quéau de Quinssy returned ashore and secretly arranged with the settlers for the arrest of all the deportees. This was efficiently executed at dawn the next day at a gun signal from the ship. The Etablissement was suddenly invaded by a group of settlers and their blacks who had mustered during the night at the home of the settler Mondon. At the wharf de Quinssy read a proclamation to the deportees, which stated that in view of peace preliminaries which were taking place between France and England and the expected alteration of the status of the Seychelles the Colonial Assembly of Mauritius had decided that the deportees would be taken to Anjouan, a land of plenty, close to active trading posts.

Deportees Moved Again

Only thirty-two of the sixty-six deportees on Mahé, together with Serpolet and the three negroes who had been sent to Frégate, left on the *Le Bélier* for there was not enough space on board to accommodate all of them. The selection was carried out by de Quinssy and a committee of thirty settlers. The thirty-four remaining deportees were taken back ashore and put under the custody of eleven soldiers left by the *Le Bélier*.

The *Le Bélier* left on 18 March to the great relief of the settlers. It was only on 31 March, however, that it reached Anjouan, after a most trying voyage during which the locked-up deportees suffered intensely from the tropical heat and the extremely cramped conditions on board.

As the then Sultan of Anjouan was reluctant to accept responsibility for the thirty-six men whom the French Republic thought would be 'useful' to him in his quarrels with his bellicose neighbours and with the Malagasy, they were not allowed to land until 3 April. In a letter to General Magallon the Sultan finally thanked him for the presents and for the 'troops' he had received and assured him that they would be treated as brothers and friends.

What treatment did the deportees actually receive at Anjouan? First they were not permitted to live within the precincts of the town but were allowed to build a cottage outside its walls. They had only just finished it and were contemplating building an obelisk to commemorate their stay on the island, when one of them, Gerbeaut, died in agonising pain on 26 April. Then Nicolas Paris and Rossignol died on 28 April, Jean-Louis Grosset on the 29th and Jean Dupont on the 30th, all in great pain. Four deaths in five days! After two days' respite more deaths followed, those of Louis Moreau, J. B. François Gorget, Jacques Brabant, Bouin, Ambroise Marconnet, Mamin, Bertrand Lacombe, Saint-Amant and Pierre Lefèvre. On 9 May five of the still healthy deportees, Pachon, Lagéraldy, Vauversin, Magnian and Jean-Marie Grosset, ran away. More deaths followed. Six weeks after landing, only seven of the thirty-three deportees remained, of whom four were already ill. The three remaining healthy deportees disappeared but the four who were ill recovered and two of them, Lefranc and Sonnois, returned to France in 1803, shortly after Vauversin, one of the five who had run away on 9 May. It is believed that all the deportees who died did so from a poison administered on the order of the 'brotherly' Sultan.

Of the thirty-four deportees who had been left at Mahé, several escaped on calling ships, including the two Linage brothers, who became prosperous merchants in the Portuguese colony of Mozambique and eventually settled at the Cape, while others, including Boniface and Pépin-Desgrouhette, died on the island. One deportee, Jacot-Villeneuve, was allowed to go to Reunion Island (then Ile Bonaparte) in 1806. In the following year fourteen of them were also allowed to go to Mauritius. Four of these, with Jacot-Villeneuve from Reunion, were to return to France when Mauritius had been conquered by the British. With the three who had managed to return to France from Anjouan and one of the Linage brothers they were the only nine deportees of the original seventy who saw France again. Jallabert, Cardinaux, Chevalier, Guilhémat and Quinon finally remained on Mahé. These five, with the ten who remained in Mauritius, eventually became British subjects, having declined to return to France. One of them, Quinon, still has descendants in the Seychelles. Pointe and Baie Chevalier, on Praslin, have probably been named after another of them.

On the renewal of the first capitulation in 1801, de Quinssy obtained a valuable concession from Captain Macadam of HMS *Sybille* : the undertaking that in future the five vessels of the small Seychelles merchant fleet would be permitted to pass unmolested through the blockade which the British navy was imposing on Mauritius, provided they flew a Flag of Capitulation bearing the words 'Séchelles Capitulation' in white on a blue background. De Quinssy apparently argued that since, after the renewal of the capitulation, the Seychelles were an English possession, its ships should not be interfered with by the British navy. This concession continued until the end of the blockade in 1810, and is reported to have been of considerable detriment to British interests and of enormous advantage to the Seychelles.

While holding the helm at the Seychelles and doing his best, by placating the enemy, to prevent an occupation of the islands, de Quinssy must have been hoping that the Seychelles would eventually be French again through a final French victory. This hope was shattered by the British occupation of Mauritius and its dependencies, including the Seychelles. De Quinssy learned about the capitulation of Mauritius on 23 December 1810 from the English vessel *Les Frères* and he was officially notified of it on 21 April 1811 by Captain Beaver of HMS *Nisus*. As the British had decided to occupy Mauritius, at least until the end of the hostilities, arrangements had to be made by them for the island's civil administration and that of its dependencies. De Quinssy was told by Captain Beaver that the English flag was to be flown on all occasions and that he must prepare a detailed plan for the administration of the Colony. To evade what would thus amount to a formal occupation of the islands de Quinssy argued that since the Seychelles had already capitulated to the British, the terms of the Mauritius capitulation were not applicable and suggested that the existing arrangement should continue. This was of no avail, as Captain Beaver, while agreeing to de Quinssy continuing temporarily in the administration of the Colony, left in the Seychelles a British figurehead in the person of the wounded Lieutenant Bartholomew Sullivan, of the Royal Marines, who thus became the first British Commandant of the Seychelles. So ended forty years of French rule and so began over 160 years of English administration.

Saddled with Colonies

The English had occupied Mauritius and the Seychelles not to acquire any new bases in the Indian Ocean, since they already held key ones such as Trincomalee in Ceylon and Cape Town to name but two, but to put an end to the effect of French privateers on English shipping and to thwart a new French move towards India, which could be anticipated from Bonaparte's expedition in Egypt. That England did not wish to retain Mauritius and the Seychelles is borne out by the fact that during the *pourparlers* of the Treaty of Paris she proposed the return of the islands to France in exchange for the few remaining French possessions in India. The proposal was rejected by France. The English found themselves saddled with colonies they did not want but their responsibility to administer. Hence the kind of 'passive imperialism' adopted towards the new colonies by the Colonial Office whose main anxiety appears to have been to avoid them becoming an economic burden to the new mother country. As a result, under the British rule the Seychelles entered into a period of long, peaceful, semi-oblivion.

The gradual upgrading of the posts of the British officials who have administered the Colony since 1810 reflects the slow but constant growth in importance of the territory and its progressive detachment from Mauritius. There were two commandants from

96

1811 to 1813, three civil agents and commandants from 1814 to 1838, four civil commissioners from 1839 to 1867, five chief civil commissioners from 1868 to 1888, three administrators from 1889 to 1902 and seventeen governors and commanders-in-chief from 1903 to the present day. It was on the appointment in 1903 of the first governor and commander-in-chief, in the person of Sir Ernest Bickham Sweet-Escott, who had also been the last administrator, that the Seychelles obtained, under Letters Patent, the full status of a British Crown Colony. Previous constitutional advances had occurred in 1872 with the appointment of a Board of Civil Commissioners with financial autonomy from Mauritius, and in 1888 with the appointment of the first nominated legislative and executive councils. The Seychelles had, however, to wait until 1948 to have their first legislative council elections in which four representatives of the landed class were elected under a new constitution, and until 1967 to obtain adult universal suffrage and a governing council with a non-official majority. The only tie which still exists with Mauritius is through the judiciary, for the Colony's appeal court for civil cases is still in Mauritius.

Slavery Abolished

The most important social event which occurred in the Seychelles after the British took over was undoubtedly the abolition of slavery in 1835. Although the newly-liberated slaves at first refused to work the land which they associated with their slavery, they eventually returned to it and fitted into a paternalistic social system with the landowner as the *paterfamilias*. However, because of the too intense fragmentation of the land and to miscegenation, which started at the time of slavery and flourished afterwards, this system has now almost disappeared and, in its place, in spite of poverty and other socially-inhibiting factors, there has evolved a community of agricultural workers, fishermen, artisans, small land owners and government employees loosely but fondly united by their language, nationality and religion. Thus, while there are class distinctions in the present Seychellois society and although the Seychellois range from the almost pure black to the almost

97

pure white, they can nevertheless be said to constitute a nation. This nationhood status in Seychelles, where there are little or no racial or colour prejudice, is one of the finest achievements of the small, poor but cheerful islands.

The abolition of slavery, which was promulgated on 1 February 1835, did not take place until 1838, for the liberated slaves had first to undergo a period of apprenticeship under their previous masters to train them for their new life and to enable the settlers to reorganise their labour force. The transitional period, originally intended to be for six years, did not produce the expected results and was repealed by proclamation on 11 March 1838. On that date all the former slaves, numbering about 5,000, were freed. The event which was resented by the settlers (although they received financial compensation from the British Government at the rate of £60 14s 3d for an adult slave) presented the Colony with a major crisis, for, almost overnight, the settlers were without a labour force. In the long run the change in the agricultural pattern of the colony brought a successful shift from the growing of labour-intensive field crops to the more profitable plantation crops such as coconut.

A Missionary Arrives

The next notable event in historical terms was of a spiritual nature. It was in the unexpected arrival in 1851, on board the *Joséphine Loizeau*, of a Roman Catholic missionary, the French capuchin priest Father Léon des Avanchers. His arrival produced great enthusiasm among the bulk of the population, which was Catholic. As the British government had hitherto turned a deaf ear to repeated petitions from the settlers for Catholic priests (apparently in the hope that the population would eventually adopt the state Anglican religion), the arrival of Father des Avanchers, who had been brought from Aden by Captain Labury, the master of the *Joséphine Loizeau*, was a minor victory for the settlers. While the civil commissioner of that time, Robert William Keate, considered what action to take, Father des Avanchers began instructing, baptising and performing marriage ceremonies

98

among the people who thronged to him. Frightened by the enthusiasm of the population, dreading Father des Avanchers' influence on the settlers and fearing an uprising the commissioner refused him permission to stay on the grounds that he was not a British subject. To the grief of the Seychellois Father des Avanchers left three weeks after his arrival. He returned to the Seychelles two years later, however, having received permission to do so after petitioning the Governor of Mauritius, his his ecclesiastical superiors, the Colonial Office and even Queen Victoria. Father des Avanchers is fondly remembered by the Seychellois Catholics as being the precursor of the highly esteemed Catholic Mission of the Colony, which was founded in 1851.

Landslide Disaster

On the night of 12 October 1862 occurred the first and only natural catastrophy in the annals of the Colony. It was a large landslide which swept through Victoria and still lives in the memory of the inhabitants of the Seychelles as the 'Avalasse'. This term, for which there does not seem to be an equivalent in the English language, well describes what took place. A large part of the town was suddenly overwhelmed by a powerful torrent of mud carrying everything before it, boulders, trees, houses, livestock and men. The death roll, believed to have reached one hundred, was never fully assessed, since apart from those who were washed out to sea many were buried. The origin of the sudden and violent storm which caused the landslide, and whose centre appears to have been above the hills overlooking Victoria, is still a matter for speculation, as the Seychelles are outside the cyclone belt of the Southern Indian Ocean. This is how an eyewitness, Lieutenant Colonel L. Pelly of HMS *Orestes* which was in harbour, described the phenomenon :

It so chanced that, during the week I passes in Port Victoria, waiting on board Her Majesty's steam-frigate *Orestes* for the mail, the Seychelles were visited by a violent hurricane, the first ever experienced there. This circular storm strengthening out of the South-East trade, veered Southward, Westward, and gave us its full fury from North West and finally subsided into the South East trade again, followed by floods of rain. I do not remember to have ever heard any sound so mournful as the Titanic sobbings of that hurricane—now hushed an instant, as, spent with passion, the tempest gasped for breath.

During the storm there were reefs all around us within a few hundred yards, and the shore was not a mile distant; yet we could see neither land nor reef, nor even sea, but only a scud of foam blown past the side like lace rapidly unrolled. On the storm subsiding, the scene ashore was melancholy indeed. The steeper hill-slopes had been washed bodily down into the valleys; in some instances crushing, during the night, estates, families and houses in one common grave and ruin. The brook by Government house had burst its banks, and poured in a torrent down the main street of the town, hurrying houses, provisions, men, women, and children along its flood towards the sea. Trees were torn up by the roots; the palm tops were twisted off at the neck, as during the cannonade at Mohamera; and the French Religieuses were crushed into the earth as they stood with their priest and their scholars at morning prayer in their hospital. I left one day afterwards; but even then some fifty people were asserted to have been killed or severely maimed, and it was assumed that some fifty more were missing on the island of Mahi. The little schooners were crunched together and sunk.

So impressed were the Seychellois by this terrifying occurrence that it became a time mark, local events being henceforth identified as having occurred so many years before or after the 'avalasse', and that it acquired *droit de cité* in the local vernacular in the saying 'Fous mois déhors, laisse l'avalasse traîne moi' ('Kick me outside and let the landslide take me'), whereby old disgruntled people still express their dissatisfaction at being neglected by their children.

Another ordeal, this time man-contributed, beset the Seychelles in 1883, in the form of a virulent smallpox epidemic, which is still remembered as 'La Vérette'. Introduced by a Seychellois who had returned to the islands from Zanzibar and undiagnosed at first by the Colony's doctors, the epidemic caused a panic. People fled to the mountains, shops and offices were closed and plantations deserted, while church bells tolled for the dead. Mahé was put in quarantine by Madagascar, Mauritius, Reunion and Aden, provisions ran out and prices rose to famine levels. According to Fanny Barkly, the wife of the then chief civil commissioner of the Seychelles who saw the effect of the outbreak, which ran its course from the middle of 1883 to the middle of 1885, hundreds died and thousands were disfigured. The disease was first diagnosed by a newly-arrived doctor from Mauritius who had been quarantined on Long Island while the epidemic was unidentified on Mahé.

Among the less dramatic, but nevertheless notable events of the British period, have been the arrival of a succession of political deportees, the accession of the Seychelles to the full status of Crown Colony in 1903, the two world wars and the general elections of 1967 and 1970.

A Barless Prison

Due to their isolation in the Indian Ocean and to their healthy atmosphere, the Seychelles have proved throughout their history to be an ideal barless prison for undesirables from both France and England. To many of the exiles who were fortunate enough to be sent to the Seychelles the sunny islands and their smiling inhabitants must have appeared as a pleasant, although at times protracted, holiday in a little world apart.

The Jacobins who arrived in 1801 were followed some three-quarters of a century later by the first British deportees in the persons of the ex-Sultan Abdullah Khan of Perak and his retinue. Twenty-five years later, in 1900, arrived one of the most colourful exiles whom the Seychelles has received, the ex-king Prempeh of the Ashanti, with a retinue of fifty-five; he was joined in 1901 by another group of Gold Coast deportees, which included seventeen chiefs and two queens. Also in 1901 arrived two Uganda kinglets, Mwenga, the Kabaka of Buganda, and Kabarega, the King of Bunyoro. Eighteen years passed before the arrival of the next exiles—three members of the American Watchtower Bible and Tract Society of Nyasaland. In 1920 came a lone exile, Mahmood Ali Shirrey, ex-Sultan of the War-sanghi Tribe of Somaliland. The following year, 1921, saw the arrival of a self-styled Sultan, Seyid Khalid bin Bargash, Preten-der to the Sultanate of Zanzibar, and his retinue of twenty-one. Then, in 1922, the Seychelles received Saad Zaghul Pasha of Egypt and four members of his cabinet.

In 1933, another batch of deportees arrived. It consisted of Ali bin Ahmed Fadh and five other members of collateral branches of the Abdali family, from Aden. In 1937, the Seychelles received Hussein Fehri Effendi Al Khalidi, of the Palestine Arab Higher Committee, and four colleagues. Then, in 1956, Arch-bishop Makarios of Cyprus arrived with three other Cypriot deportees. The last exile to be sent to the Seychelles was Afif Didi of Gan island, Addu Atoll, one of the nineteen atolls of the Maldives. He arrived in the Seychelles in 1963 after his abortive attempt to secede Addu and the neighbouring atoll of Suvadiva from the central Maldivian Government at Malé. The best remembered of recent 'reluctant' visitors to the Seychelles is Archbishop Makarios. His arrival, in March 1956, with Bishop Kyprianos of Kyrenia, the Rev Stavros Papathangelou and Mr Polycarpos Joannides, all from Cyprus, caused a sensation in the Seychelles. The deportation of the Archbishop and of his com-panions followed the Eoka, or Union with Greece, movement in Cyprus, which was accompanied by a wave of terrorism.

The deportees were housed in the Governor's Lodge at Sans Souci overlooking Victoria. It was from this vantage point that the Archbishop and the other deportees were able to see the arrival of the Duke of Edinburgh, on 16 October 1956. In his book 'Birds from Britannia', the Duke recalls his visit :

> For various reasons the outward journey began by air to Mombasa in Kenya, where I joined the Yacht on 16 October. Our first call was at the Seychelles islands in the Indian Ocean; not flat coral reefs but great jutting heads rising blue-green out of a brilliant sparkling blue sea. Archbishop Makarios was undergoing a period of compulsory retirement there at the time. I didn't meet him then, but when five years later he came to

Buckingham Palace with the other Commonwealth Prime Ministers, he reminded me of the visit and told me that he had watched some of the proceedings from his house.

The deportees were at first unable to communicate with members of the public without written permission from the governor of the Seychelles. At the beginning of June, however, they were put on parole and could then circulate and speak to whoever they liked. They were released on 28 March 1967 and on 6 April left on the Greek tanker *Olympic Thunder*, which had been diverted to the Seychelles to take them aboard.

In a letter to the local newspaper, *Le Seychellois*, Archbishop Makarios wrote : 'I have visited many places all over the world and it is no exaggeration to say that the Seychelles islands contain the most beautiful places I have ever seen—perhaps the Creator willed that they should be so isolated so that the primitive natural beauty He created should not be destroyed.'

On 31 August 1903 the Seychelles ceased to be dependencies of Mauritius and acquired the status of a British Crown Colony. This event, which followed repeated requests from the inhabitants of the Seychelles for a larger measure of autonomy from Mauritius, was a welcome step. With the new status the Seychelles could look forward to constant, if slow, progress. The fiftieth anniversary of this event was celebrated in Seychelles in 1953.

The two world wars made little impact on the isolated and remote Seychelles. During the first years of World War I life was barely ruffled in the Colony. Towards the end of 1916 however, at the request of Lieutenant-General Smuts, the Commander-in-Chief of the British East African Forces, a Seychelles labour contingent eight hundred strong was recruited and sent to East Africa. The request had been for five thousand labourers accustomed to head transport and general work, experienced in wharf and stevedore work. The contingent reached Kilwa Kisiwani on Christmas Eve. It returned five months later, however, having lost forty-one per cent of its strength by disease, especially bacillary dysentery and malaria which were unknown in the

Seychelles and against which the men had little or no natural resistance. Another World War I event which brought the realities of war to the door of the Seychelles, was the presence in local waters of the Germain raider *Koenigsberg*, which is reputed to have taken refuge in the lagoon of Aldabra atoll in November 1916 and drove a number of scared ships into Port Victoria.

Similarly, apart from acute shortages of imported goods, the Seychelles suffered no real hardship from World War II. The Colony saw the arrival on Mahé of the Fourth Heavy Battery of the Ceylon Garrison Artillery; of the Third Indian Garrison Company; a Royal Air Force wireless station and the departure of the two Seychelles companies of the Royal Pioneer Corps whose two thousand men saw action in Egypt, North Africa, Palestine and Italy.

POLITICAL AWAKENING

If the year 1965 saw the advent in Seychelles of party politics, when the newly-formed Seychelles People's United Party defeated the Seychelles Democratic Party in a by-election in the Praslin and La Digue islands constituency, it was only in 1967 that the people of the Seychelles really awoke to politics. In that year, for the first time in the history of the Colony, general elections were held on the basis of adult universal suffrage and a legislative council was elected with a majority of non-official members. Up to then the main opposition to the colonial government had been through the Seychelles Taxpayers' and Producers' Association, which represented the landed class and which had won the four non-official elected seats at the 1948 general elections, the first legislative polling to be held in the Seychelles. The STPA also managed, under restrictive franchise, to win against independent candidates a majority of the elected non-official seats at all subsequent legislative council elections.

During the intensive campaign for the 1967 elections both the Seychelles People's United Party and the Seychelles Democratic

Party campaigned for approximately the same social reforms, but differed about the future political status of the Colony. While the Seychelles Democratic Party demanded integration of the Seychelles with Britain, the Seychelles People's United Party wanted only an association. Although the Seychelles Democratic Party obtained some five hundred votes fewer than the Seychelles People's United Party at these elections, it obtained four of the eight elected non-official seats of the new legislative council, against three to the Seychelles People's United Party and one to an independent candidate. It therefore emerged as the majority party.

New Form of Rule

Under the new constitution there began what could be called 'Committee Rule', since four committees of non-official members of the council were made responsible to the whole council for separate aspects (social services, agriculture and natural resources, public works and communications, and finance) of the administration. The chairmen of the committees were respectively the leader of the Seychelles Democratic Party; the leader of the Seychelles People's United Party; the independent member of the council and an official member of the Council, the Financial Secretary.

The new constitution had been intended as a transitional one, to give non-official members of the Council experience in public administration. In 1968 both parties declared the new constitution to be impractical, since it entailed no 'responsible' government, and in 1969 demanded a new constitution. Following the visit of Lord Shepherd, Minister of State of the British Government, in August 1969 and the constitutional conference held in London at the end of that year, the Seychelles were granted a constitution based on the English model. It became operative with the 1970 election. This election contested by both main parties and by two new small parties (the Parti Seychellois and the Seychelles Christian Union) was won by the Seychelles Democratic Party, this time with a comfortable majority. It obtained

105

ten of the fifteen elected seats of the new Legislative Assembly, and the other five seats went to the Seychelles People's United Party. After the elections the latter party declared itself in favour of independence.

Since the new constitution was based on a ministerial system of government, the leader of the Seychelles Democratic Party, James R. Mancham, became the first Chief Minister of the Seychelles, while the leader of the Seychelles People's United Party, France Albert René, became in fact if not in name the leader of the Opposition. The Seychelles, however, are still a Crown Colony, one of the few remaining, whose Governor has important reserve powers and the direct control over foreign affairs, internal security, finances, civil service and the official press and radio.

Page 107 (*above*) School children of the Seychelles. The many racial types do not seem to inhibit friendship; (*below*) family scene on Desroches island

Page 108 Carnival scenes: (above) young boys enacting *Treasure Island*; (below) school pageant group representing the early Christians' struggles in Rome

A ROMAN SCENE
IN THE DAYS OF
SAINT AGNES

7 THE PEOPLE OF THE SEYCHELLES

THEIR ORIGIN

THE Seychelles society, which has evolved peacefully and harmoniously from people originating from Europe, Africa, Madagascar, China and India, is an outstanding achievement in racial relationships. The major ethnical contribution has been from the Africans, who formed the lowest but largest stratum of society when the islands were first settled.

Although miscegenation started at the time of slavery, it appears to have been speeded up after the slaves were freed. In the early population censuses of the Colony the inhabitants of the Seychelles could be classed according to their racial origin, but this was no longer possible by 1911 because the races had become so mixed.

While miscegenation must have been due to some extent to the lack of colour and race prejudices of the French, another important factor must have been the gradual impoverishment and accompanying loss of status of the land-owning class due to intense land fragmentation and also to the precipitous topography of the granitic islands, which lent itself to crops adapted to the miniaturisation of agricultural estates. The fragmentation has been caused by the old French succession law (still in force in Seychelles) under which the estate of a deceased is inherited equally by all his heirs. Thus arose a community of poor and illiterate whites, better known in the Seychelles as 'vieux blancs' or 'blancs rouillés', who could not have been averse to intermarrying or mating with mulattoes or blacks.

Out of the mixture has evolved a wide range in colour but a distinct people with common and usually lovable characteristics.

G

THE SEYCHELLES

The average Seychellois is a dark coloured man of medium size and, usually, European features. His shortcomings are natural indolence and inclination to live from hand to mouth, but he is cheerful, loyal and extremely clean. The Seychellois, however poor, is always neatly dressed and even the poorest of cottages are always spotlessly clean. Although heavily influenced by the French language, culture and outlook, he is also proud of his British nationality and is also very much attached to his Roman Catholic religion, to such an extent that the language, nationality and Catholicism of the Seychellois can be said to have been, in ascending order, their main unifying factors.

STRUCTURE OF THE LANGUAGE

According to the 1960 population census, the home language of ninety-four per cent of the Seychellois is creole, the French patois of the Colony, but as creole is close to French, the latter is widely understood in the Seychelles.

It has been said by Suzanne Sylvain about the French creole of Haiti:

> We are in presence of a French language moulded in an African syntax, or, as languages are usually classified according to their syntaxic origin, an 'éwé' language with a French vocabulary.

This definition of the Haitian creole, equally applicable to the other French creoles of the world, is too rigid, since, according to Elodie Jourdain, the syntax of the French creole patois is a mixture of both African and French elements. The transplanted Africans who coined these patois not only took from French whatever words they needed to express their thoughts, but also used the most fitting French or African 'tools' to link these words together. The Seychelles creole, like the Mauritius creole, to which it is closely allied, is made up basically of a French vocabulary with a few 'creolised' Malagassy, Bantu, English and Hindi words and a mixture of Bantu and French syntaxes. However, some of the most curious words of French origin spring not from modern French, but from dialects of south-west France or from

110

nautical terms and show that the original settlers were mainly sailors from the French maritime provinces.

As with the other French creoles, the Seychelles creole is ornate and colourful, but it has some shortcomings. It has no orthography, being only spoken, and it cannot be used to express abstractions. Because of these shortcomings, creole does not deserve the status of a distinct language. It is, however, a charming means of expression, which because of its picturesqueness and poetic appeal to the imagination is unlikely to die out in the Seychelles. Being particularly suitable for story telling and for singing, especially in the plaintive mood, creole also plays an intrinsic and popular part in the islands' folklore.

HABITS AND CUSTOMS

If the creole patois has a mixed French and African origin, other habits and customs of the present Seychellois can be said to be either of pure French or pure African origin.

The Seychellois' fear of the supernatural, which expresses itself in superstitious beliefs, can be ascribed in the first place to their African ancestry. That such beliefs have succeeded, in spite of over a century of Christianity, in permeating the whole Seychelles society can however be related to poverty and insecurity for which superstition is but a form of escapism. The beliefs lead to harmless practices whose object is to protect suppliants from the evil eye, to obtain favours or to retaliate in presumed cases of 'malfaisance' or hostility. The protective or aggressive talismans, or charms, better known as 'grisgris', consist of small packets, of an inch or two, which according to Burton Benedict contain objects such as small bits of iron, cooked food and various other items which are carried by the suppliant or are put in the way of the bed clothes or the washing utensils of the intended victim so that he may come in contact with them.

The witch doctors, better known as 'bonhommes' or 'bonne-femmes du bois' or again 'donneurs' or 'donneuses de bois', use simple and varied divining techniques, such as a pack of cards, pebbles, seeds, pieces of wood, tea or coffee strainings, or a mirror, and use ambiguous expressions to induce their clients to choose their own victim or presumed enemy. After a first consultation, the witch doctor may ask for time to determine the nature of the 'malfaisance' and at the second consultation may declare that it has been caused by a 'cochonnier' or 'gonages', or undefined dirty object, which has been buried, say, under the doorstep of the client. The witch doctor then claims that he has removed the object, probably with the help of a spirit or 'dondosia' or zombie, and he produces it.

Witch doctors are sometimes herbalists with wide reputations as healers. The most famous herbalist cum 'donneur de bois' of the Seychelles was Charles Zialor, better known as Dialor, who died at over ninety years of age in 1962. Dialor's reputation was so extensive that it is said that even doctors have occasionally advised patients whose ailments they could not diagnose or cure to 'try Dialor'. In an ordinance enacted in 1958 (Ordinance No 4 of 1958), the Seychelles Government tried to stamp out sorcery in Seychelles. Although there have been prosecutions and convictions, witch doctoring is as widespread as ever. The answer to these practices undoubtedly lies in improved social and economic conditions.

Social Problems

Another social disability, the so-called amorality of the Seychellois, may also be related to African ancestry and also to the present poverty and feeling of insecurity among the people. The main reason usually given for the large number of 'ménages' or temporary and free unions, which result in a large number of illegitimate births (about fifty per cent of the total number of births every year), is the Seychellois's sense of decorum and craving for prestige which, for instance, impels a girl not to marry unless her parents and those of her fiancé have saved enough money for the traditional lavish wedding feast. It is equally true that the girls who prefer to live 'en ménage' rather than wait for marriage may be driven to this course for other reasons. But the prevalence of temporary unions is not a new event in the Seychelles society, but an heritage from the past, from the time of slavery and of the early days of settlement when no priests were available. It might even be traced back to the original African society from which the slaves came and in which there was almost certainly no place for prolonged celibacy, especially among women. That the teachings of the Church have not yet been able to overcome this problem may be ascribed to long-prevailing economic conditions in the Seychelles and not necessarily to an inborn amoral sense.

Old Customs

An African custom which has survived to this day is the popular communal dance known as 'moutia'. It is a nocturnal gathering around a fire, and is accompanied by the throbbing beat of the African drum. The dancing consists essentially of feet Shuffling in couples, the men and women dancers facing each other a few feet apart. 'Moutias' are also usually accompanied by a melopoeia, very often improvised, which is either a lament, the narration of an event or a satire aimed generally at some important member of the audience. Although 'moutias' are more frequent in the outlying islands, whose unsophisticated environment is probably more congenial to such gatherings, they may sometimes be seen or heard on Mahé, even in the suburbs of Victoria, and are then a reminder that Africa is neither too far away nor completely suppressed in the Seychellois' mixed temperament.

Other customs may be ascribed to the European ancestry of the Seychellois. Two of them, the 'sérénade' and the 'levée de chambre', belong to the nuptial lore of the Colony. The third one, the ever popular 'contredanse', is a country dance.

The 'sérénade', which used to be much more frequent, is the picturesque nuptial procession of newly-weds to their wedding feast. It is invariably accompanied by musical instruments, one or two violins and a triangle, which precede the newly-weds, while the parents, friends and other guests follow them. In the old days when there were no motor-cars in Seychelles, 'sérénades' used to follow long tracts of countryside and must have looked very colourful as the pealing music, the shy bride and bridegroom and the formally but gaily-attired guests wound their way over the hills to a homestead. Nowadays when there is a 'sérénade', which is not often, the newly-weds usually leave the bridal car to join the procession only a short distance away from the house in which the reception is to be held.

Old, extremely flowery, romantic and traditional wedding songs, better known as 'romances', and speeches in French, usually recorded in old copy-books, survive, but all this charming and poetic lore is unfortunately disappearing and will soon live only in the memory of the older people.

The 'levée de chambre' is a curious custom which must have originated in the old French countryside and is still practised. It consists of a visit paid by the parents to the bride and bridegroom on the day following their wedding to establish the bride's purity —which is the invariable finding. A cake, similar to the wedding cake, is usually cut and eaten on the occasion and shouts and fireworks proclaim the happy news to the neighbourhood. The 'levée de chambre' is also a reminder of the old days when guests had to travel long distances on foot or by boat to attend wedding feasts, which consequently lasted one week or more.

The 'contredanse', which is a 'danse commandée', also stems from France. It is usually danced to the lively tune of violins and of a triangle, which is an essential accompaniment. After the choice of lady partners the dancers face each other in two lines and, at the injunction of a 'commandeur', execute a series of graceful and sometimes intricate figures. Introduced by the early settlers, the 'contredanse' has a noble origin. It is reported to have been a regular feature at the court of the 'Sun King', Louis XIV. The 'contredanse' is the most popular dance of the Seychelles. It is a special feature of 'camtolés' or country dances.

THE PEOPLE OF THE SEYCHELLES

Apart from a few large farmers, senior government employees and recent expatriate settlers, mostly British, Seychelles' society is composed of the families of agricultural workers, fishermen, artisans, small farmers and junior government employees, who constitute the backbone of the country.

The Seychellois family or 'ménage' is usually made up of the father, the mother and an average of five children, among whom may be 'enfants soignés', or adopted children, and one or two aged relatives. Although the father is the wage earner, he occupies only a peripheral role in the family and the mother is its focal point. The man is expected only to pay the rent for the house and to provide food and clothes for the family. The strong mother-child tie of the Seychellois family is illustrated by the love and respect with which the mother is commonly surrounded and the indifference which is often shown to the father. An old woman is thus never completely forsaken in the Seychelles, while old men are sometimes entirely alone. Little respect is also shown by grown-up children to their father.

BASIC FOODS

The Seychellois's staple food is rice imported from Burma, and fresh fish caught around the islands. The Seychellois is also very fond of what he calls 'gros manger', that is roots and tubers like cassava and sweet potato, plantains, especially the variety known as St Jacques, and breadfruit. For economic reasons, he consumes relatively little bread and milk and scarcely any eggs.

The favourite meat of the Seychellois are turtle meat (which is now unobtainable since the capture of the green turtle has been prohibited) and pork. The latter is especially liked and a fat pig is usually slaughtered for weddings and other feasts. A pig is kept by every household in the Seychelles as a form of saving. The Seychellois is generally very fond of animals and keeps a variety of pets and farm animals, which wander about in the 'cours' or courtyards of the households, and include cats, dogs, ducks, rabbits, guinea pigs and, sometimes, giant tortoises. As a result, the yelping of innumerable dogs at night and the crowing of a large number of cocks at dawn are characteristic of the Seychelles.

Beef and poultry are generally eaten only by the well-to-do. Young salted 'fouquets' or shearwaters, which are cropped before the fat young birds are due to leave their underground nests, and fresh tern eggs gathered on the egg islands are also relished during the cropping season. Occasional treats are also provided by the octopus which is speared in the shallow lagoon waters and is cooked in a variety of ways, and by the frugivorous flying fox, which is either shot or caught at night and is usually curried. Unlike the Mauritian and the Réunionnais, the Seychellois does not however eat tenrec, the small hedgehog-like wild mammal from Madagascar which has been introduced in Seychelles and is often seen at night when it creeps out of its burrows to feed.

The Seychellois also eats surprisingly few vegetables. His favourite vegetables are in the form of 'brèdes', which are soups made of the green leaves of cultivated and wild plants, and 'chatinis' or chutneys which are usually made from green fruits like mangoes, golden apples and 'billimbis', the fruits of a tree related to the carembola and which look like gherkins, and are eaten with the rice, fish and meat.

The favourite fruit of the Seychellois is undoubtedly the banana, of which there are no less than 25 types in Seychelles. Mangoes, pawpaws, 'fruits de cythère', or golden apples, and pineapples are also popular. The ubiquitous coconut, as could be expected, plays a large part into the diet of the Seychellois. Coconut oil is commonly used as cooking fat and for soap making, while coconut milk extracted from freshly grated coconuts, is widely used for flavouring curries, stews and sweets.

Among the delicacies which are usually consumed by the well-to-do and are served to visitors are avocado pears which are particularly tasty in Seychelles, crayfish, crabs, the savoury fresh water shrimp, or 'camaron', 'palmiste', which is obtained from the apical bud of the coconut palm and of the wild 'palmiste' palm and which provides what is usually called the millionaire's salad. To obtain a 'palmiste' a mature, old palm, must be felled. The young, furled leaves of the 'langue de boeuf', or birds-nest-fern, are served as a salad, and there is the unique, delicate nutty flavoured jelly of the green coco-de-mer nut which is usually served as a dessert with a dressing of liqueur.

Seychelles Fashions and Leisure

The elderly women of the Seychelles still wear the dignified nineteenth-century cotton 'casaque' or blouse, with a long skirt and a foulard tied with a knot at the back of the head, while the elderly men wear long cotton trousers with or without jackets, and shorts, with a large leather belt which it is fashionable to tighten very low in front. Some old men still wear small ear rings, a reminder of the old sailing or piracy days. The young, however, have adopted the latest European fashions which reach the islands in about six months.

Football is the national game of the Seychelles, but boat racing and 'goggling' (underwater swimming) in the clear, warm water of the coastal lagoons are also favourites with the more fortunate. Dancing and, more recently, the cinema also have a strong appeal to the young as well as to older people.

For everyone there are fishing, dominoes and 'matouloumba', which is a popular game of cards, drinking 'bacca' and toddy, the local beers made of sugar cane juice and of the sap of the coconut palm. Perhaps more than anywhere else in the world, the people enjoy yarning about the good old days. . .

8 LAW, RELIGION AND LANGUAGE

A CCORDING to Article 8 of the Capitulation of Mauritius to the British forces on 3 December 1810, the religion, laws and customs of the inhabitants of the colony were to be safeguarded. Four years later, under the Treaty of Paris, France ceded Mauritius and its dependencies (and therefore the Seychelles) to Britain. As there was no special provision in the treaty concerning the religion, law and customs of the Mauritius and Seychelles settlers, it has been contended that with the coming into force of the treaty the terms of the capitulation ceased to have any legal force.

Lord Godrich, the British Minister for the Colonies, declared in a despatch to the Governor of Mauritius on 3 August 1831 that with the final cession of the island the terms of the capitulation had become a mere matter of history. The same view was also upheld by the French Chamber of Deputies on 2 March 1833 when it declared that the Treaty of Paris had annulled the deed of capitulation of 1810. The latter declaration was made in connection with a petition from some Mauritian settlers who were opposed to the abolition of slavery and who had appealed to the French government against what they considered to be a breach of the terms of the capitulation. Lord Derby, a successor to Lord Godrich, expressed an opposite view and confirmed the validity of the capitulation terms.

From 1878, the Union Catholique of Mauritius tried to obtain an increase in the subsidy which the British government was paying to the Catholic diocese of Mauritius and, to support its request, referred to the terms of the capitulation. This move was opposed by the representatives of the Anglican diocese of the island. They

118

contended that the terms of the capitulation had been superseded by those of the Treaty of Paris and were no longer applicable. The heated debate which ensued induced William Greene, an English jurist who had settled in Mauritius, to study the status of the Catholic Church there. The outcome was a thoroughly documented work which established that the terms of the capitulation had not been affected by the Treaty of Paris and that England was therefore still morally bound to conform to them. It was the despatch to the British Minister for the Colonies of a copy of this work by Governor Pope Henessy, a Catholic who supported the claims of the Mauritian Catholics, which caused the following statement to be made by Lord Derby, in a despatch dated 14 March 1884 :

> Nor do I see any reason for questioning what is the actual effect and extent of the 8th article of the Capitulation, or for doubting that it retains its validity.

It is therefore to Article 8 of the Capitulation which may be attributed the status and the survival of the French law and language in Mauritius and the Seychelles and of the Roman Catholic religion in Mauritius. Since there was no established church in the Seychelles at the time of the capitulation, the Catholic Church had no special status there. This induced the British government to attempt to substitute Anglicanism for the Catholicism of the Seychelles settlers during the first half of the nineteenth century.

RELIGION : CATHOLICS AND ANGLICANS

Probably because of the troubled times and also of the small population of the islands, no priest was made available to the inhabitants of the Seychelles during the forty years of the French rule. The settlers, the majority of whom were Catholics, therefore lapsed into a condition of religious ignorance by the time of the capitulation, while the slaves, many of whom were heathens, were in an even worse situation.

The Anglican Church, which was under the patronage of the

119

British Government, had a clear field. It was only in 1843 that an Anglican priest was appointed to the Seychelles in the person of the Rev George Delafontaine, who was Swiss. Before that, the Seychelles had been visited by two Anglican priests from Mauritius, a Mr Morton, who arrived in 1832 and who became the first civil chaplain of Seychelles, and the Rev Languishe Bank in 1840. The foundation of the Anglican Church on the islands is owed to Mr Delafontaine. He was, unfortunately, violently opposed to the Catholic Church and by his intolerance antagonised the settlers. When he left the Anglican Church had made little progress and the first Catholic missionaries had already arrived. The Anglican Church never regained the lost opportunity, and today Catholics outnumber Anglicans by ten to one.

The attempt to substitute Anglicanism for Catholicism in the Seychelles was made during the administrations of the civil commissioners Charles Augustus Mylius and Robert William Keate. Mylius, who administered the Seychelles from 1839 to 1850, is reported to have been sympathetic to the settlers' repeated requests for Catholic priests and to have supported their requests on two occasions in 1849. The main reason for the dilatoriness of the British government in granting the requests was obviously the wishful thinking that the inhabitants of the Seychelles would eventually adopt the Anglican religion. Another reason which, according to Webb, may have caused further dilatoriness was the popular outburst in England in 1850 against the so-called 'Papal aggression', when the Pope set up territorial bishops in England. News of the event must have reached Mauritius at the time when a decision about the sending of Catholic priests to Seychelles could no longer be delayed and it may have then tinged the attitude of the authorities there.

Keate, who was the nephew of an Anglican bishop and who succeeded Mylius, appears to have been less tolerant. Keate believed that since the larger number of the inhabitants of the Seychelles (the released slaves and mulattoes) were not Catholics, but heathens, it would be strange if they were allowed to be converted into a foreign church rather than into the Anglican one.

He also believed that the conversion of the settlers to the Anglican faith was only a matter of time. He appears to have formed this opinion on the visit in Mahé, in 1850, of the Anglican Bishop of Colombo, when a number of Roman Catholics accepted his ministrations. However, shaken the following year by the popular enthusiasm which accompanied the visit of Father des Avanchers and by the sorrow of the islanders at his departure, he finally forwarded a petition from the settlers to Mauritius requesting a priest to be sent to Mahé. The year 1853 saw the arrival of two Catholic priests, Fathers Jérémie and Théophile of the Savoie Capuchin Province. They were followed by other priests and, in due course, by nuns of the order of St Joseph of Cluny and by teaching brothers of the Christian Instruction. As Webb puts it, the Roman Catholic Church had come, had seen and quickly conquered.

The Seychellois of today, Catholics and Anglicans alike, in spite of lapses, are very religious. The churches are full on Sundays and on religious feast days. Very few Seychellois, if any, die without the ministrations of their priests. The latter, as well as the nuns and religious brothers, are also esteemed and respected by all.

THE LAW

Judiciary

Today there is a Supreme Court and two magistrates' courts in the Seychelles. The Supreme Court consists of a Chief Justice and a Puisne Judge. The Appeal Court for criminal cases is in England and that for civil cases is in Mauritius.

Civil and Criminal Law

Before 1805 the law of the Seychelles consisted, according to Bradley, of that of the old French East India Company; of laws promulgated by the King of France from 1766 to 1790 (after the royal French government had 'bought back' Mauritius and Reunion from the company) and the edicts published by the

121

Colonial Assembly at Mauritius from 1790 to 1803. Today the law in Seychelles is based on the French civil codes and on English criminal law.

The French codes (civil codes, code of civil procedure and code of commerce), which are generally known as the Napoleonic Codes, as modified by local legislation, constitute the common civil law of the Seychelles. They came into force in 1805 under the governorship of General Decaen, the then Captain-General of the French establishments beyond the Cape of Good Hope. In 1815 after the cession of Mauritius and its dependencies to England, they also became the law of these islands by virtue of a proclamation of Sir Robert Townsend Farquhar, the first British Governor of Mauritius.

The French penal code of 1810 became the criminal law of the Seychelles, in a similar way, in 1838. In 1904 a consolidated Penal Code of Seychelles was instituted in order to embody the many amendments which had been made from 1838 to 1903. In 1952, however, a completely new code of criminal law, based on English law, was enacted. At the same time the existing criminal procedure code was amended and consolidated.

Opposition to Change

The change of the criminal law based on the original French code to that based on the up-to-date English criminal law was not without opposition. The bill was first moved at the meeting of the Seychelles Legislative Council of 1 February 1951. In moving it, Mr Ernest Bernard Simmons KC, the then Attorney General of the Seychelles, remarked that the penal code, as it existed, was a mixture of French and English law, consisting of not more than two-thirds of French-Roman law and of one-third of the common law prevailing in England, the USA and in parts of the British Commonwealth, and that the code contained elements derived from the penal code which had been in force for one hundred years previously. Speaking on behalf of the four elected members of the Legislative Council who were opposed to the bill, Mr Gustave de Commarmond, the member for Praslin and La Digue, asked whether the bill could be adopted without contravening the act of capitulation and stated that the penal code was not the obsolete, antiquated curiosity which it was considered to be in some quarters, but to his colleagues and himself it was a living reality, the operative force of which had been upheld in the Supreme Court of Mauritius in 1902 and 1932. He claimed that the local legal profession had not been consulted about the bill which appeared to be the sole work of Sir Charlton Adebert Gustavus Lane, the Law Revision Commissioner.

The decisions of the Supreme Court of Mauritius referred to by Mr de Commarmond were incidental acknowledgements of the validity of the terms of the capitulation. Mr de Commarmond finally moved that the reading of the bill be postponed for four months to give an opportunity for local lawyers to study it. In replying to Mr de Commarmond's speech, the Attorney General made the surprising statement that the Act of Capitulation was not actually an act, but a temporary treaty which existed before the Treaty of Paris and that the terms of the capitulation were not law at all. Mr de Commarmond's amendment was put to the vote and carried. The reading of the bill was postponed once more at the meeting of the Legislative Council of 21 June 1951, to enable a committee of local lawyers to consult an impartial authority. The new code was finally adopted without opposition on 29 April 1952, on the recommendation of the committee of lawyers who had received the advice of Sir Sydney Abrahams, a member of the British Privy Council.

LANGUAGE

The Seychellois creole patois has even been transplanted to East Africa, where it is spoken by the thousands of Seychellois, including second and third Kenya born generations, who live there. Those among them who returned to the Seychelles after the independence of Kenya were able to communicate with their countrymen and to settle back in the Seychelles without much difficulty.

The other languages spoken in the Seychelles are French and English. According to the 1960 population census, French is the home language of five per cent and English that of one per cent of the population. Although French is the mother tongue of five times as many educated Seychellois as is English, there has been a slow but gradual decline in the knowledge and use of French in the Colony during the last thirty years. The main reasons for this have been the increased importance given to the teaching of English in schools and the marked decline in the standard of French teaching. In 1944 English was substituted for French as the medium of instruction in all schools of the Colony, while French continued to be taught as a 'foreign' language. It was hoped that by being taught in a language completely different from their native creole, the young Seychellois would be less confused and would therefore make quicker progress. In 1970, however, nearly thirty years later, the change having failed to produce the expected results, it was decided to teach only English in the first three years of primary schooling and to give extra teaching time to French when it is introduced in the fourth standard. Only time will tell whether this new step has been in the right direction and if it will produce a general improvement in the generally low standard of primary education in Seychelles and provide a satisfactory knowledge of both English and French to primary school leavers.

French is the second official language of the Colony and may be spoken in the Legislative Assembly. It is largely used for legal deeds and is also the language of the churches, being solely that of the Roman Catholic and Seventh Day Adventist Churches and, in part, that the Anglican Church. It is also used in part of the press, for all the newspapers, except for the official Government *Gazette* and *Seychelles Bulletin*, are bilingual. French is also the language which the average creole-speaking Seychellois is naturally inclined to use on formal occasions, such as for the inter-island greetings which are broadcast every day over Radio-Seychelles.

Page 125 (right) Good Cause appeal at a carnival. Note the placard in English and Seychelles Creole patois; (below) a Mahé girl smells a flower in the botanic garden

Page 126 (above) Praslin island has a botanical wonder in its Vallée de Mai, the only place in the world where the coco-de-mer palm grows in numbers; (right) the extraordinary coco-de-mer nut

9   AGRICULTURE AND INDUSTRY

THE Seychelles are excluded from the large world fish markets by their remoteness and isolation in the least frequented of the oceans. They have no oil or mineral resources and have had to rely almost entirely on agriculture to subsist. The crops grown successfully on the islands during the last two hundred years are among the most exotic ones and include foodcrops, cotton, coconut, vanilla, cinnamon, patchouli and, lately, tea. Coconut has been by far the most important one.

The earliest, although minor, industries of the Seychelles have exploited the islands' natural resources, such as timber, tortoises and turtles, whales and bird guano, but these assets, as in so many tropical lands, were quickly exhausted. Another early 'industry', in which Seychellois shipowners engaged during the first years of the nineteenth century, was the slave trade. The incomplete picture we have of these early industries shows that although they were insignificant in terms of the Indian Ocean or even of the Mauritius trade, they were important to the small and the then still thinly populated islands.

TIMBER PRODUCTION

On 23 July 1796 Captain Hulet, of the French ship *Le Neptune*, declared in Mauritius that he had left the Seychelles on 3 June with a cargo of a hundred tortoises, 24,000ft of timber, cotton and a little coconut oil. The timber was one of the many loads exported from the Seychelles from the middle of the nineteenth century to the beginning of the present one and which contributed to the disappearance of the magnificent and irreplaceable rain forests which covered the islands. In the old sailing days timber was as important as iron is today. It was the indispensable material which enabled the great European powers to compete with each other on the world's seas, hence the strong interest which the timber resources of newly discovered lands created. The Seychelles forests were gradually depleted for the export trade and by the needs of the local shipbuilding industry. Shipbuilding was for many years the main industry of the islands.

From 1773 to 1810, fifteen ships are recorded to have transported substantial cargoes of timber from the Seychelles to Mauritius, where wood was scarce because of extensive and indiscriminate deforestation and where the excellent Seychelles hardwoods found a ready market in the shipbuilding industry. The most valued of these timbers were 'takamaka' for framework and curves, 'gayac' and 'bois de table' for planking and wales, 'bois de natte' for masts and 'bois marais à petite feuille' for yards and bows. During the French period alone, that is until 1810, some 300,000 to 500,000ft were probably exported. An even larger quantity must have been exported during the early part of the British administration, since timber exploitation and export continued well into the first quarter of the present century.

Data about the shipbuilding industry are incomplete and fragmentary, but it is known that in 1808 the Seychelles merchant fleet had nine ships, of twenty-six to seventy tons burden, all constructed on the islands. After the British conquest shipbuilding appears to have made further progress. From 1810 to 1861 the construction of forty-eight ships, amounting to 4,605 tons, is recorded, but it was not the total output, for according to Toussaint this must have amounted to some seventy-five vessels. During the same period, the Mauritius output appears to have been over four times as large as that of the Seychelles in terms of numbers, but not more than double in terms of tonnage. These figures do not include the smaller craft such as fishing boats which were built for use around the islands. Some of these ships sailed the world's seas and became known far and wide. A small ship-building industry survives in the Seychelles today. It builds schooners, fishing and racing boats, including the graceful, flat-bottomed 'pirogues', which are constructed by skilled craftsmen in open-air yards with carefully-selected timber.

Shipbuilding's Origin

The first ship to be built in the Seychelles was probably the *Créole des Seychelles*, of forty-five 'tonneaux', which called at Port-Louis, Mauritius, presumably on her maiden voyage, on 5 November 1791. The most remarkable ship to be built in the Seychelles during the first half of the nineteenth century was the *Thomas Blyth* of 372 tons. Constructed by Crook and Naz at Anse Louis, on Mahé, it was purchased on the stocks for £2,000 by James Blyth, an English merchant of Mauritius, who named it after his father. It was the first unit of a fleet of some fifty merchantmen which belonged to the house of Blyth in Port-Louis. They became known as the 'pea soupers' because of the shade of yellow they were painted.

The *Thomas Blyth*, which arrived in Mauritius in July 1837, on the completion of her maiden voyage from the Seychelles, was one of the few Seychelles ships to have crossed the Atlantic. Most of the others appear to have been used for trade with Madagascar, India and Australia. Two of them, the *Arpenteur* of ninety-five tons, and the *Joséphine Loizeau* of ninety-four tons, were sold in Port Adelaide, Australia, and a third one, the *Marie Laure* of 328 tons, was sold in Hobart, Tasmania. The latter, a sister ship of the *Thomas Blyth* which has been described as the last-but-one of the Mauritian barques, at one time traded for the Blyths between London and St Helena. She finished her days on the banks of the river Yarra, near Melbourne.

TORTOISES AND TURTLES

Originally, giant tortoises, green turtles and hawksbill turtles abounded on and around the Seychelles. The giant tortoise, except for a small number of domesticated individuals, has been exterminated, but the green turtle and the hawksbill turtle survive in greatly reduced numbers. This is especially true of the green turtle, whose population in the Seychelles waters has reached such a dangerously low level as to preclude its survival even under strict protection.

Up to the year 1800 giant tortoises appear to have been the most important export of the Seychelles. They were shipped by the hundreds to Mauritius to be used as food. From 1782 to 1789, for instance, no fewer than 1,103 tortoises were carried on nine ships. According to Toussaint at least ten thousand to twelve thousand tortoises must have been exported from the Seychelles from 1773 to 1800. These figures do not take into account the tortoises which were poached, levied by warships or consumed locally. By 1800 the giant tortoise population of the Seychelles was practically exhausted. Tortoises exported after that date probably came from Aldabra. Today it is difficult to estimate the original tortoise population of the Seychelles. That it was a huge one, numbering at least tens of thousands, can be inferred from the recent survey of the tortoise population of the arid atoll of Aldabra by the Royal Society. This is of the order of 100,000.

The green turtle is the large marine animal of soup fame. It owes its English name to the colour of its fat. It shares with the manatee and the dugong the ability to browse in shallow tropical waters and to eat their marine vegetation. The green turtles of the Seychelles, like those throughout the world, travel hundreds of miles from their feeding grounds to 'ancestral' island beaches to mate and breed.

Although green turtles were originally so plentiful around the granitic islands that anyone could go out in a boat to spear one whenever it was wanted, it is around the islands of the Aldabra group (Aldabra, Assumption, Cosmoledo and Astove) that it existed in truly great numbers. This group of islands, according to Parsons, has seen the greatest concentration of breeding turtles in the Indian Ocean in modern times, or perhaps at any time.

130

It is to these islands that great fleets of green turtles, several thousand strong, repaired to breed every year from December to April presumably from their feeding grounds of the Mozambique Channel. After years of decimation by man these great fleets have been reduced to a meagre rearguard which is itself threatened with extinction.

Food For Ships' Crews

Ships which sailed from the islands or called there took a heavy toll of the turtle population for the meat was believed to cure scurvy and because, like the giant tortoise, the green turtle can live for days or weeks without food and water it provided a continuous supply of fresh meat for the crews. When green turtles became scarce around the granitic islands they had to be fetched from the outlying coral islands, especially from the Aldabra group. The regular exploitation of turtles on that group of islands started in 1906 when they were first cropped for 'calipee'. This is the dried semi-cartilaginous tissue joining the carapace (upper shell) of the green turtle to its plastron (breast-covering) and is used in the turtle soup industry to give 'body' to the soup. Its production involves a great waste of turtle meat for a 200–300lb turtle yields only about three and a half pounds of 'calipee'. All 'calipee' produced in the Seychelles was exported and the export figures show the heavy toll taken of the turtle population during the last sixty years. In 1912, which appears to have been the peak year for 'calipee', 36,900lb valued at £2,140 and the equivalent of nine thousand turtles were exported. From 1907 to 1938, 375,560lb valued at £61,849 and the equivalent of some 114,000 turtles were exported. During the next 30 years, with the gradual decline of the turtle population, only 144,789lb valued at £29,735 and the equivalent of some 40,000 turtles were exported.

As regulations put into force in 1925 to preserve the eggs and young of the green turtle, and in 1948 to impose close seasons for catching adult green turtles, proved ineffective the Seychelles government declared a complete ban on the capture of green turtles in 1968. Only time will tell whether this measure has come too late.

Tortoiseshell

Another early enterprise of the Seychelles was the tortoiseshell industry, for as far back as 1786 de Malavois wrote that from 1,000 to 1,200lb of tortoiseshell were being taken annually from the Seychelles. The tortoiseshell of commerce comes from the smaller 'caret' or hawksbill turtle. Unlike the green turtle, the hawksbill turtle is not eaten in the Seychelles where its flesh is reputed to be poisonous. Also, unlike the green turtle, the hawksbill is more numerous around the granitic islands than around the outlying coral ones.

Commercial tortoiseshell consists of the polished imbricated plates of the turtle. When they are not disfigured or badly worn they are prettily mottled, usually in reddish-brown or dark brown on a light yellow background. A special pale-coloured shell, sparsely mottled and with cloudy fleckings of pale reddish-brown, is obtained from the Cosmoledo and Alabra turtles. This particularly beautiful shell is attributed to the fact that the carapace of the turtles of these atolls is usually covered by a thin crust of lagoon mud. There are thirteen plates in the carapace of the hawksbill turtle and plates of thin yellow horny material, the 'yellow belly' of trade circles, under its body. Tortoiseshell is especially valuable commercially because it can be 'slabbed', that is pressed and welded to the desired thickness without any apparent joint. It is usually graded for colour. The finest grade is the 'demi-blonde', an orange coloured shell without mottling. It was from this grade that the casket which France presented to Queen Elizabeth II on her coronation was made. The second grade is an even red, referred to as Seychelles red. The third has a reddish mottle while the fourth has a good open mottle. The poorest grade is a dark coloured shell. Highly polished and beautiful articles are made from tortoiseshell by Seychelles craftsmen.

Some 134,000lb of tortoiseshell, valued at £13,000 and the equivalent of some 45,000 tortoises, were exported from 1893 to 1968. The largest export year was 1919 when 8,825lb were sent overseas. Recent exports have been of the order of one to two tons a year.

THE WHALING INDUSTRY

The whale industry in the Seychelles started towards the begining of the last century. Both American and English whalers were attracted by the Sperm whales which were found in the vicinity of the islands. The fishing grounds appear to have been off Denis and Bird islands and the whales, which are generally in schools of one to ten, are reported to have been especially numerous around the Seychelles in July and August. As the whalers, sail or steam, could not go very far out to sea (the oil had to be extracted from fresh whales) stations were set up on Ste Anne island opposite Port Victoria.

American whalers, who preceded the British in Seychelles waters, had a whaling station on Ste Anne for about seventy years. American whaling, according to Davidson, was greatly curtailed in Seychelles in 1867 when a large number of ships were destroyed in the Sea of Okhotsk by the Confederate battleship *Shenandoah*. The last American whaler visited the Seychelles in 1904.

British whaling appears to have started in or about 1823. In 1827 there were seven British whalers in the vicinity of the islands and after a gap between 1870 and 1914, during which practically no whaling was undertaken, a British firm, the St Abbs Whaling Company, established a large factory on Ste Anne island. Its liquidation in 1915 put an end to whaling in Seychelles. The disappearance of the industry is attributed mainly to the fall to uneconomic levels of the price of Sperm whale oil.

It is recorded that in 1879, during a four-month period, two American masters sent 2,400 barrels of oil from Port Victoria and that from October to December 1913 115 whales were captured near the Seychelles and 122 from October to July 1915. The only contribution which the whaling industry made to the economy of the Colony was in the form of custom duties on the oil shipped from Port Victoria.

BIRD GUANO

Another small but worthwhile industry has been that of quarrying bird guano. Seychelles guano is a useful phosphatic fertiliser formed from the accumulated droppings of the hordes of sea-birds which are believed originally to have arrived in the southern seas during the last glacial age. It contains an average of fifty-five per cent tricalcium phosphate. Being only slowly soluble to plants, this form of phosphorous is especially suitable for tropical soils which are rich in iron and aluminium, since these soils readily combine with soluble phosphatic fertilisers and make them un-available to plants.

The Seychelles guano industry appears to have started in or about 1895. The central islands of North, Aride, Frégate and Bird and those of the Amirantes, were the first to be quarried. In 1905 a local company was formed to exploit the guano of the outlying island of St Pierre, of the Providence group. Ex-ploitation appears to have started on Assumption in or about 1910 and on Astove, both of the Aldabra group, in 1927. The only Seychelles islands on which guano is still quarried are those of St Pierre and Assumption where some relict deposits are left. There is now little or no guano on the central granitic islands or on those of the Amirantes.

Seychelles guano was first exported to Mauritius and later to New Zealand, East Africa, Reunion, South Africa and India. Mauritius still is the main market for this fertiliser. It is used for manuring sugar cane plantations. Nearly one million tons of guano, worth some £1½ million, have been shipped since the inception of the industry. The greatest benefit the Colony has derived from it has been the continued employment on the out-lying islands of hundreds of indentured workers from the central granitic islands.

AGRICULTURE AND INDUSTRY

THE SLAVE TRADE

The slave trade in Seychelles, which was based on the buying of slaves on the East African coast, mostly at Mozambique and to a lesser extent in Madagascar for sale in Mauritius and Reunion, appears to have started in 1803 and to have lasted to the end of the French period. What probably induced Seychellois ship-owners to join the trade was the fact that these were war years and that the Mascarene slavers were unable to supply the market in Mauritius and Reunion. After the British occupation of Mauritius the trade stopped or dwindled rapidly.

According to Toussaint, eleven Seychelles ships were engaged in the trade during the most active period and they are estimated to have carried 1,016 slaves to Mauritius in twenty-two voyages. These figures obviously do not include the unrecorded voyages or the slaves who were landed in the Seychelles. The slave population of the colony increased from 1,820 in 1803 to 3,015 in 1810. Also according to Toussaint losses on the way must have been of the order of twenty-one per cent. From 1803 to 1810 two hundred slave cargoes were received in Mauritius and the contribution of the Seychelles to the Mauritius slave operations during that period was about ten per cent.

TWO PERIODS OF AGRICULTURE

This history of agriculture in the Seychelles can be divided into two periods by the year 1835 when slavery was abolished. The first period, which started with the original settlement in 1770, was mainly devoted to production of food-crops. The second period has been devoted mainly to growing less labour-intensive plantation export crops such as coconut, vanilla, cinnamon and patchouli.

Although the main object of the first settlement of the Seychelles was the growing of spices, the settlers had to grow food-crops to feed themselves and their slaves. These crops consisted of maize, rice and roots. The food-growing acreage increased

135

from 221ac in 1788 to 2,502ac in 1810, while the population increased from 257 to 3,467. So the Seychelles were able to become ships' victuallers.

The only other crop to have been grown on a plantation scale during this eariy period was cotton, which found a ready market in Mauritius. The boom years for this crop appear to have been from 1805 to 1820. The area under cotton increased from 666ac in 1803 to 2,757ac in 1810, and in 1818 exports valued at 150,000 US dollars, and which consisted mainly of cotton, were sent to Mauritius. Cotton growing made some people rich in the Seychelles, but competition from America was too strong and by 1822 its production had practically ended. Based on slave labour (one fed slave was estimated to be able to produce one bag of cotton per year) it vanished with the abolition of slavery.

Coconut Growing

At first the settlers do not appear to have paid much attention to the coconut, but later they worked hard to extend its cultivation. It was being widely grown in 1850 and in 1898 it constituted the main crop, with clove and vanilla ranking second and third. From 1909 to 1914 100,000 coconut palms were planted. An intensive planting campaign reached its peak in 1930. The last part of Mahé to be planted was in the extreme south and the last granitic islands to be cultivated were probably the smaller ones of the Praslin group, such as Félicité, Marianne and Les Soeurs. Although planting on the coral islands started later, it was carried out more quickly. Peak production was reached in 1964, when more than seven thousand tons of copra, worth £488,000, were produced for export. According to the 1960 Agricultural Census Report, there are 23,000ac under coconut in the Seychelles.

At first the coconut crop was crushed locally and the oil was exported to Mauritius, where it was sold on the local market, or to Ceylon to be shipped by tanker to the United Kingdom. From 1902 onwards, the copra trade grew at the expense of that of oil, the copra being exported to Marseilles in France and Hull in England. From 1894 to 1905 considerable exports of nuts and soap were also made, the nuts being sent to Mauritius and Aden and the soap to Zanzibar and Madagascar. From 1931 to 1949 the United Kingdom was the main market for Seychelles copra. It was only in 1951 that exports of copra began to India, which now buys practically all the islands' exportable production.

Although coconut-growing made steady progress many problems had to be faced. In addition to economic slumps, especially during World War I and in the 1930s, the industry has its problems of disease and insect pests. The most damaging pests have been the sap-sucking scale insects, which have now been controlled by biological means, and the melittomma borer, which is unique.

Scale insects were recognised to be a noxious pest of coconut in the Seychelles in the 1920s. Attacks by these insects, which must have been introduced accidentally, reached serious levels. Infestation became so intense and widespread that the coconut palms turned black and the islands appeared to be in mourning. The blackness of the palms was due to the secretion on the coconut leaves (on which the scale insects lived) of a 'honeydew' which allowed the growth of 'fumagine', a black, sooty mould. The mould was found fouling even boulders and buildings. The problem was solved in the late 1930s by the introduction of the coleopterous 'ladybirds', which were previously practically non-existent on the islands. They fed on the scale insect and in a few months the situation was controlled. The suppression of scale insects in the Seychelles constitutes an outstanding success of biological control, and it has led to a mean annual increase of some two thousand tons in the Colony's copra crop.

A Unique Pest

The problem presented by the melittomma borer, which is a small brown beetle found only in the Seychelles and in North-West Madagascar, has been more formidable. What is most curious and baffling about this insect is its distribution; although it occurs on certain granitic islands, such as Mahé, Praslin and Silhouette, it

137

does not occur on the other granitic islands or on the coral ones. This distribution has been attributed to the fact that some species of wild palms known to be the natural hosts of the beetle do not (or did not) occur originally on the uninfested granitic islands and on the coral islands.

That the melittomma did not spread to these islands can be attributed to the fact that the adult insect lives only two or three days and that the gravid and very heavy female beetle can scarcely fly. The damage is done by the larva of this beetle, which as soon as it hatches out bores into the bole of the coconut palm and feeds on its sap. Some nine to twelve months later the larva emerges as a beetle which dies shortly after mating and laying. After repeated infestations coconut palms become hollow at their base and are finally blown down.

Although melittomma was discovered in the Seychelles in 1903 it was only in the 1950s that serious attention was given to controlling it. No predator or parasite of melittomma is known, so no biological campaign could be waged against it. Instead, a campaign was launched on an island-wide scale. This involved the tedious and painstaking treatment of every infested tree, by gouging out the necrotic, infested tissues and coating the healthy exposed ones with a mixture of creosote and Stockholm tar. The campaign was started in 1960, and has largely succeeded.

The islands' copra, which is of excellent quality, comes from the long, narrow and most adaptable Seychelles coconut, which the settlers found on their arrival and which they subsequently planted all over the islands. This nut, unlike those from many other coconut-producing areas, falls as soon as it is mature. The muffled sound of the dropping nuts is one of the characteristic and comforting sounds of the Seychelles plantations at night.

Orchid Vanilla

The commercial vanilla pod is produced by three species of orchid, the only ones to be grown on a plantation scale. The most intensively grown is *Vanilla planifolia*. The others are *Vanilla tahitiensis*, which produces the Tahiti vanilla, and *Vanilla pom-*

138

pona, which produces the 'vanillon', or Guadeloupe vanilla. The first species originates from Mexico, where it is a wild climbing plant of the tropical forests. It has been introduced into a number of tropical lands, such as Madagascar, Reunion and the Seychelles. Madagascar is at present the largest producer of vanilla in the world.

In its native Central America, vanilla is usually pollinated by bees of the genera *Melipona* and *Trigona* and by humming-birds. When vanilla was introduced into other parts of the world it was more of an ornamental plant than a commercial one for its flowers, whose reproductive organs are protected by a hood or cap, could not pollinate naturally. The Belgian botanist Charles Morren was the first to pollinate vanilla artificially in 1836, but the simple method now used in most vanilla-producing countries, including the Seychelles was discovered on Reunion Island in 1841 by a young slave named Edmond Albius. The method consists of lifting the protective hood or cap with a match-sized piece of wood and pressing the exposed stamen on to the stigma below. Pollination by hand must be carried out every morning, for the newly-opened vanilla flowers wither if left unfertilised for more than a few hours. Pollination of vanilla is usually carried out by women and children, whose light touch is suitable for this delicate work.

Vanilla was introduced into the Seychelles from Reunion in about 1866. The first export, of 110lb, appears to have been made in 1877. Towards the end of the last century vanilla cultivation expanded rapidly and for several decades brought great prosperity to the islands. As vanilla was then grown on the share-cropping system even ordinary labourers reaped large crops and earned substantial amounts. From 1890 to 1903 the Seychelles exported as much vanilla as Bourbon (now Reunion) which was one of the earliest producers, and more than all the other British colonies in total. In 1901, the export was more than seventy tons, valued, even then, at some £70,000. By 1929, however, due to disease and to the advent of synthetic vanillin, exports had fallen to some twenty tons and they declined rapidly afterwards. During recent years production has fluctuated between half a ton and seven and a half tons.

Compared with the six to eight hundred tons' production of Madagascar, the present Seychelles' average production of five to six tons in a good year is insignificant. However, for the tiny islands of Praslin and La Digue, (not even marked on many world maps) where the Seychelles crop is grown almost exclusively it has been a major source of income.

Cinnamon Exports

When vanilla cultivation collapsed, the Seychelles settlers, or planters as they were then known, were able to turn to another plant, which had been introduced in 1772 and which had invaded and covered the deforested slopes of Mahé. It was cinnamon, one of the cherished spice plants of Pierre Poivre.

The first cinnamon product to be exploited in the Seychelles was the bark of the then existing trees. In 1908, 1,202 tons of cinnamon bark were exported. By 1915, however, all the large cinnamon trees had been felled or stripped of their bark and production had fallen to some two hundred tons. It declined further during the following years, but recovered in the 1940s. This recovery, due to the short supply of cassia bark from the East, especially from China and Indo-China, resulted in the export of 3,059 tons, worth some £561,000 in 1968. In that year, for the first time in the history of the Colony, cinnamon produced more revenue than the main coconut crop.

When cinnamon bark began to fail the planters turned to cinnamon leaf oil which is distilled from the fresh leaves of the cinnamon plant and which is used to manufacture synthetic vanillin. The production of cinnamon leaf oil rose from fifteen tons in 1916 to about a hundred tons in the 1950s. Recently, due to a shortage of cropping labour, the production of cinnamon leaf oil has fallen back to the 1915 level.

Although cinnamon is exploited on four of the twenty-eight granitic islands of the Seychelles, it is only on Mahé and Silhouette, which are the highest and rainiest islands, on which

140

it is abundant. On Mahé, which accounts for the bulk of the cinnamon products of the colony, it is the dominant species of the secondary vegetation which cloaks the higher and middle slopes and it occurs also as an intercalary undergrowth in the coconut groves of the lower slopes, and even of the calcareous coastal flats.

Cinnamon, which has for many years been the second most important crop of the Colony, may aptly be said to be one of God's gifts to the Seychelles. It was introduced by a genial plant lover and imaginative administrator, and has not only helped to preserve the mountainous slopes of the largest islands as they become deforested and exposed to the tropical rains, but also, although self-planted and scarcely tended, has provided a means of livelihood for thousands of islanders from the beginning of this century.

Patchouli from India

Although patchouli is a native of the Philippines, it has been grown in India from time immemorial, and has been used there in the form of dried leaves for keeping moths and other insects from costly shawls and silks. It is because of costly Indian shawls, which were distinguished by their odour of patchouli, that Europe became familiar with the plant. The secret was discovered by French manufacturers in the 1850s. They imported dried patchouli leaves to give the Indian perfume to their own products. Patchouli appears to have been introduced into Britain in the days of the English East India Company. Patchouli oil was at first considered to be a distinguished perfume and was used in Court circles, but it eventually came to be looked down upon as the 'Bad Woman's' perfume.

The essential oil obtained from the leaves of the herbaceous patchouli plant is still used in perfumery. It is considered to be one of the best fixatives for the heavy types of perfume like Amber, Chypre and Fougère, and it is also used as a soap perfume. It blends well with geranium, clove, vetiver, cassia and other essential oils used in the soap industry.

141

It was towards 1915, following the successful distillation of cinnamon leaf oil, that patchouli was thought of as a possible crop in the Seychelles. Production started in the 1920s. Until 1951 the only patchouli product to be exported from the islands was oil. In that year, however, dry patchouli leaf was also exported for the first time and it is in this form that the very large part of Seychelles patchouli is exported today.

Seychelles patchouli competes on the world's essential oil market with 'Singapore' patchouli, which is produced mainly in Malaysia and Indonesia. The Seychelles product enjoyed a great boom from 1943 to 1947, when Asian territories were over-run by the Japanese. During these five years, the golden age of the golden oil, patchouli became the second in importance of the Seychelles crops, fetching undreamed-of prices. At the peak of the boom, in 1946, one litre of patchouli oil which in pre-war days was worth some Rs 6 (or 50np), brought as much as Rs 550 (or some £82) on the local market. A forty gallon drum of oil was worth £5,000. The boom caused old ladies to uproot their rose trees to grow patchouli and even inspired a local merchant to use patchouli as currency. He offered a new motor-car for so many litres of oil.

Although the production of patchouli has now fallen to pre-war levels and is but a fraction of that of the boom period, it continues to be a useful peasant crop which in times of scarcity and high value can be grown quickly and becomes a precious revenue earner, especially to small farmers.

The latest of the plantation crops of the colony is tea, which is being grown on the higher slopes of Mahé, where it is promising. It is hoped eventually to produce enough tea for the local requirements and for a sizeable export. But the Seychelles are now turning towards tourism which it is fervently hoped will become a thriving industry.

Page 143 left: (above) The most curious Seychelles pitcher plant; (below) the fruit of the jelly-fish plant of the Seychelles, which has been described as a 'living fossil'

(below left) a female leaf insect; (below right) the giant tenebrionid beetle of Frégate island

Page 144 Public works: *(above)* the Rochon dam, completed in 1969, is the first of a series of schemes planned by the Seychelles government to ensure water supplies; *(below)* Seychelles airport, here seen under construction, was completed in 1971 and can receive the largest passenger planes

10 COMMUNICATIONS AND SERVICES

Sea and Air

U NTIL recently, the only way to and from the island world of the Seychelles was by sea. Connection with the outer world, apart from cables and radio telephone, consisted of bi-monthly calls of British and Indian steamers plying between India and East and South Africa and of occasional cargoes from the United Kingdom, Singapore, South Africa, Kenya and Mauritius. For visitors to the islands this meant long and usually inconvenient transits either in Mombasa or Bombay. The slow route through East Africa or India is still the traditional one to and from the Seychelles.

In 1963, however, the United States Air Force which had recently established a satellite tracking station at La Misère, on the main island of Mahé, started a weekly servicing flight from Mombasa with an amphibious Grumman Albatross. This little plane, which heralded the air age in Seychelles, also inaugurated the first regular airmail contact with the outer world. The first regular passenger air service to and from the Seychelles followed in 1970 from the unfinished airport which the British government was then building in exchange for the Colony's loss of sovereignty on the islands of Aldabra, Farquhar and Desroches. They had been transferred to the newly-formed British Indian Ocean Territory.

This new passenger service, operated by Air Kenya (previously Wilknenair), consisted of weekly flights from Mombasa of a small Piper Navajo aircraft. A complete air service with the outer world

I

was achieved only on 4 July 1971 when thousands of Seychellois gathered on the completed airport to watch the landing of a BOAC VC 10 to inaugurate a weekly service to and from London. On this day the Seychelles came within comfortable reach of the rest of the world, but at the same time lost the isolation which was one of their charms.

But the sea is still the major form of inter-island communication in Seychelles. Although the two larger islands, Mahé and Praslin, have good trans-island and coastal roads, the sea is sometimes the only means of access to some of the more remote homesteads on these islands. Praslin and La Digue, the most populated islands after Mahé, are also still connected with the latter by tri-weekly sailings of the ferry-boat *Lady Esme*, while Silhouette, North island and Frégate, which are run as unit plantations, are only connected with Mahé by weekly sailings of the islands' schooners. The smaller granitic islands are connected with Mahé, Praslin and La Digue by the islands' pirogues or other small craft. Connection with the outer coral islands is even less frequent and consists usually of two to three monthly sailings of copra schooners from Mahé.

Telephone, Telegraphy and Radio

Since 1954 Victoria has had a modern automatic telephone system which replaced the limited and rickety one introduced during World War II. This system is now being extended to other districts of Mahé. Soon one will be able to telephone from one end of the island to another. Inter-island communication can be carried out by radio telephone between Mahé and Praslin and La Digue. The other islands are in touch with Mahé through Radio Seychelles, which has a good island coverage, but cannot communicate with the main island and are still isolated.

Telegraphy came to the Seychelles as early as 1893 when Cable and Wireless began a cable service between the Colony and Zanzibar and Mauritius. This service is still in operation. Recently the company started an international radio-telephone service.

There are two broadcasting stations in Seychelles: Radio Sey-

146

chelles and the Far East Broadcasting Association or FEBA. The latter is a foreign station with a head-office in London. In 1970 it began to use the Seychelles as a vantage point to broadcast non-denominational Christian religious programmes in English and eight vernacular languages to Ceylon and Western India. Radio Seychelles, the Colony's own broadcasting station, started in 1941 with the assistance of Cable and Wireless, which provided the technical facilities. At first it broadcast for only one hour a week. This programme was extended to one hour a day in 1952 and to two hours a day in 1960. In 1965 the station became autonomous from the cable company and greatly extended its broadcasting time and coverage. Today Radio Seychelles is on the air three times a day, at lunch time, at tea time and in the evening, and also broadcasts educational programmes. It broadcasts mainly in English and Creole. Radio Seychelles can be heard on most of the islands and apart from the church pulpit is the only mass medium of the Colony.

Banks

The first bank in the Seychelles was the New Oriental Bank Ltd, which opened in 1887 but closed in 1892. It was followed by the Commercial Bank of Mauritius which operated from 1911 to 1915. In 1959, after a gap of nearly forty-five years during which banking transactions were carried out by the leading merchants of Mahé, a third bank started business in the Seychelles. It was Barclays Bank DCO, now Barclays Bank International Limited. Another bank, the Standard Bank, started operation in 1968. Both are in Victoria. Barclays Bank has however a part-time branch in Praslin.

Press

Because of the limited reading public, the Seychelles are not well served by newspapers and periodicals.

The first newspaper of the Seychelles, called *Le Seychellois*, appeared in 1839. It was followed by a succession of mostly short-lived newspapers, such as *L'Impartial* in 1877, *Le Réveil* in

147

1889, *Le Petit Seychellois* in 1916, *Le Réveil Seychellois* in 1924, *Reuter's Telegrams and Advertiser* in 1926, *The Clarion* in 1933, *l'Action Catholique* in 1935, *The Government Bulletin* in 1942, another *Le Seychellois* in 1943 and *l'Echo des Iles* in 1957. With the advent of party politics, three more papers saw the light : *The Seychelles Weekly* in 1963, *The People* in 1964 and *Le Nouveau Seychellois* in 1970.

Today the publication with the largest circulation (2,500) is *l'Echo des Iles*, an illustrated bi-monthly published by the Roman Catholic Mission. Of the two dailies, *The Seychelles Bulletin* and *Le Seychellois*, the former, an official paper which reproduces the BBC news, has a circulation of 1,000. *Le Seychellois*, with a circulation of 700, speaks for the Farmers' Association. Of the political newspapers, the *Seychelles Weekly*, with a circulation of 1,500, expresses the views of the Seychelles Democratic Party; *The People*, a mimeographed weekly with a circulation of 700, is the spokesman for the Seychelles People's United Party and the bi-monthly *Le Nouveau Seychellois*, with a circulation of 300, is that of Le Parti Seychellois. Most of these papers are bilingual.

Social Clubs and Benevolent Societies

The oldest social club of the Colony, the Seychelles Club, was founded in 1894 and is still strong and active. Among the other clubs are the Tobruk Club, an ex-servicemen's club established after World War II, and the more recent Rotary Yacht and Creole Clubs.

Cultural societies include the Alliance Française, which was formed in 1953; the Seychelles Society, a history and natural history society formed in 1960, and the New Seychelles Theatre Club formed in 1967 and which produces plays in English and French.

Among the sport clubs the most popular are the ones which constitute the Seychelles Football Association. The oldest football team of the Colony is Ascot, formed in the 1930s. There is also a small cricket club.

The benevolent societies include the Union Chrétienne Sey-

148

chelloise, which was founded in 1961 and has been doing out-standing social work especially in the field of low cost housing; the recently formed Seychelles Children's Society and the local Branch of the Royal Society for the Prevention of Cruelty to Animals, which was established in 1954. The Seychelles government has also recently started a Provident Fund to provide old age pensions for workers.

POSTAL SERVICES

The Central Post Office is housed in the Queen's Building in Victoria. There are also sub-post offices at Anse Royale, the largest village of Mahé; at Grand'Anse and Baie Ste Anne on Praslin, and at La Passe on La Digue. In addition there are branch post offices at the United States Air Force satellite tracking station on Mahé and on Silhouette and Coëtivy. In the villages of Mahé and Praslin (where there are also post boxes) postage stamps are sold by licensed vendors. On the outlying coral islands postage stamps are available in the small shops provided by the island manage-ments.

On the larger islands of Mahé, Praslin and La Digue, the mail is delivered by postmen who still travel on foot over the islands. The mail for Praslin and La Digue is carried three times a week by the inter-island ferry boat. That for the other islands is carried at longer intervals by the island schooners. On the outlying coral islands the mail is received only every two or three months and constitutes one of the excitements provided by the arrival of the boat from Mahé.

Before 1963 the overseas mail (including the 'air mail') came by steamers from Mombasa or Bombay. Since the creation of the direct air link with Europe, the air mail from Europe and the United States arrives on the BOAC plane from London; that from the rest of the world comes on the US tracking station weekly plane from Mombasa. Newspapers and other sea mail still come via Mombasa or Bombay and are usually about two months old when they reach the Seychelles.

THE SEYCHELLES

Postage Stamps

It is largely through their postage stamps, especially through the attractive pictorial stamps, that the Seychelles have become known to the outer world. It was only in 1890, in the reign of Queen Victoria, that the Seychelles had its first issue of stamps. Until then the Colony, as a dependency of Mauritius, had used Mauritius stamps. These stamps were cancelled by the 'B 64' obliterator, which was the distinctive colonial stamp cancellation code of the Seychelles. These first Seychelles stamps, as well as those issued during the reigns of Edward VII and George V and the first part of the reign of George VI, were what is known as 'key type'; that is they belonged to a design which was common to other British colonies, with only their name plate and value being peculiar to the Seychelles. In spite of this uniform design these stamps have great charm because of their attractive and contrasting colours. In the words of a Seychelles stamp collector they look like jewels on a page of an album.

In 1938, during the reign of George VI, the first pictorial issue was made. It depicted a fishing 'pirogue', a giant tortoise and a coco-de-mer palm. According to Farmer, their large format and pictorial design was a complete departure from the stereotyped keyplate designs which had hitherto characterised the stamps of the Colony, whilst the choice of the photogravure method was an innovation unique amongst new stamps for the Crown Colonies. Several other pictorical issues have been produced since then. They all depict a variety of island scenes or examples of the islands' flora and fauna. There was another innovation in 1969 when the latest definitive issue of fifteen stamps was devoted to local historical events. It was the first time that a whole set of stamps of the Colony had been devoted to one subject.

Many commemorative stamps have been issued in the Seychelles. The first, such as those of the Silver Jubilee of 1935; of the Coronation of 1937; of the Victory in 1946; of the Royal Silver Wedding of 1948; of the Universal Postage Union of 1949 and of the Coronation of 1953, consisted of 'key types' common to all British Colonies. In 1956, however, a set of two commemorative stamps was issued to commemorate the bi-centenary of the formal act of possession of the islands by the French. It was the first time that commemorative stamps unique to the Seychelles had been issued. The stamps depict the Stone of Possession as it then stood in the grounds of Government House in Victoria, and they were followed by several other commemorative issues recalling other local events, such as the bi-centenary of the first settlement of the Seychelles in 1770; Commonwealth events, such as the centenary of the British Red Cross Society in 1970, and even world events such as the first landing on the moon in 1969.

Although the Seychelles cannot boast of valuable stamp rarities, some of their scarce, surcharged or overprinted stamps have reached respectable values. Among them are the 1896 18 cents on 45 cents stamp with double surcharge, which is catalogued at £80, and the 1957 5 cents on 45 cents overprint, with thick bars omitted, which is catalogued at £300.

CURRENCY WEIGHTS AND MEASURES

The currency and weights and measures used in the Seychelles constitute a hotch potch of archaic and cumbersome standards.

During the French period the official currency was the 'livre tournois', which was divided into twenty 'sols', but the principal money in use was the Spanish piastre which was worth ten 'livres tournois'. Sterling currency was introduced in 1826, but with the adoption by Mauritius of the Indian rupee as its currency in 1876, the latter also became the currency of the Seychelles. This was changed to the Mauritian rupee in 1934 and the Seychelles one in 1939. The Seychelles rupee, which is worth 1s 6d ($7\frac{1}{2}$np), is divided into a hundred units or 'sous', the latter being a corruption of the old French 'sol'. Other currency terms still in use in the Seychelles are the 'vingt-cinq marqués' and the 'cash'. The first of these, which is the equivalent of 75 cents of a rupee, derives from the 'marqué' of the French period which was worth three cents of an Indian rupee and which was made in Mauritius from thin copper sheets cut into rectangular pieces and marked with the numeral '3'. 'Cash', which is equivalent to two cents of a rupee, derives from a copper currency used in the English settlements in India and which General Decaen, the last French governor-general of Mauritius and Reunion, is reported to have minted in large quantities from copper captured on prize ships.

Length is expressed in the French foot or 'pied', which is equivalent to 1·06 English feet (0·32m). Material is measured in the shops in ells or 'aunes', one 'aune' being 46·9in or 1·20m. Distance is invariably expressed in miles. Surface measurement is expressed in the old French term of 'arpent', which is equivalent to 1·043ac. From it is derived the French word 'arpenteur', surveyor. The surface is also measured in 'gaulettes', one 'gaulette' being equal to 10×10 French feet. This measure is used exclusively in the field, for allotting tasks to agricultural workers, when a 'gaulette' or 10ft long pole is used to measure out the area to be worked.

Volume is generally expressed in French cubic feet. Stacked firewood, however, is always measured in 'cordes', a 'corde' being equivalent to forty-eight French cubic feet, while for constructional work, like wall building, the old French 'toise', which is equivalent to thirty-five French cubic feet, is still sometimes used. Capacity is measured by the 'touque' which is equivalent to 22 litres. Weights are usually expressed in terms of the metric system, but instead of the kilo, the French pound or 'livre', which is equivalent to half a kilo, is generally used in the retail trade.

11

THE NOTABLE SIGHTS

AT the heart of Victoria, the old Etablissement du Roi of the French and the only town of the Seychelles, is 'l'Horloge' or Clock Tower, which is probably the most photographed feature of the town. Erected by public subscription in 1903 in memory of Queen Victoria, it is a small replica of the tower clock of Vauxhall Bridge in London. It is so well-known that it is said of a country bumpkin in the Seychelles: 'Il n'a pas vu l'horloge' —'He has not seen the clock tower.' From it radiate the roads which lead to most parts of Mahé and to the port where the ferry boat and the schooners which connect Mahé with the other islands have their moorings.

Government House

Near the Clock Tower is another well-known feature of Victoria —Government House, the residence of the governor and commander-in-chief of the Seychelles. Built in 1911 to replace the previous single-storey Government House on an adjoining site, the present double-storey house is a handsome and pleasant building. Its spacious rooms and verandas belong to the Victorian colonial era. Even today it is the scene of colourful functions; levees, cocktails and dinner parties which are reminiscent of the past days of Empire. At the end of formal dinner parties at Government House and before the ladies retire, the governor and guests stand to toast 'The Queen'. To be invited to Government House, however, one has only to sign the visitors' book, which is kept in one of the small kiosks at the gate of the Government House Avenue.

153

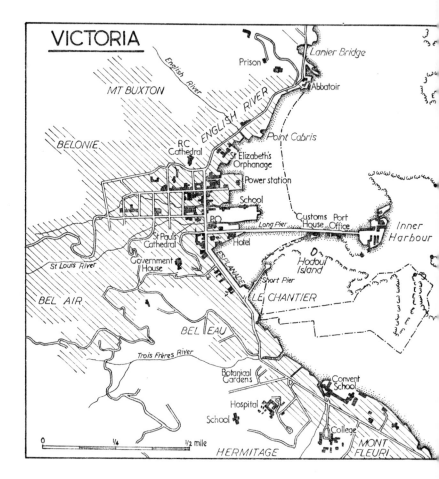

The first governor to live in the house was Colonel C. R. M. O'Brien, who administered the Colony from 1912 to 1918, and it is best seen from Quéau de Quinssy's tomb on a knoll in the Government House grounds. Nearby is the tomb of Sir John Thorp, a popular governor, who administered the Colony from 1958 to 1961, and whose death by drowning on 13 August 1961 was lamented by the whole population.

Botanic Garden

Victoria's most attractive feature is its small botanic garden. It was created in 1901 by Rivaltz Dupont of Mauritius, and it reflects the days when a newly-awakened interest in development brought the importation of numerous tropical plants from other areas. The garden, which is about 15ac (6ha) in area, is now more of a public park (the only one in the Seychelles) than a trial ground for the garden is occupied mostly by mature specimens. The visitor is usually impressed by the luxuriant growth of the trees and shrubs, the result of the equable equatorial climate and the high rainfall.

There is a collection of tropical palms, among them the six unique species of Seychelles endemic palms; striking Mascarene latans; the strange dwarf bottle palm which is endemic to the small Round Island off Mauritius; the talipot palm of Ceylon, and the colourful sealing-wax palm from Borneo. Among the flowery ornamental trees of the garden is the flamboyant, or flame tree, of Madagascar, whose gnarled trunk and branches become a dazzling red umbrella during its flowering season; the pink pouyi, whose masses of flowers resemble cherry blossom from a distance; the rose of Venezuela, a small evergreen tree whose red flowers are large, round and pendulous and glow under its dark green foliage, and the striking cannon ball tree, whose beautiful and fragrant flowers and brown spherical fruits (of the size of cannon balls) are born directly on its trunk.

Other striking trees in the garden include the breadfruit tree, a native of Malaysia and now a very common tree in the Seychelles where its fruit replaces the potato; kapok, or the silk-cotton tree; the elephant apple tree, a native of tropical Asia which produces white, magnolia-like flowers and fruits enclosed in greatly enlarged, stiff edible green sepals; the durian tree, which is a native of Ceylon and whose fruits are famous for their delicious but most unpleasant-smelling pulp, and many others.

Among the lesser, but nevertheless striking, plants of the garden are the 'traveller's tree', which is a native of Madagascar and which is grown in the tropics for the unique, ornamental appearance of its fan-shaped cluster of long leaves, and the dioecious nutmeg tree, whose ripe apricot-like fruit splits to disclose the nut. The garden also has a giant tortoise pen with specimens of giant tortoises from Aldabra, and aviaries in which there are specimens of the orange-breasted flying fox of the Seychelles.

Other Town Features

Other points of interest in the town include the Roman Catholic Cathedral of the Immaculate Conception, which like all the old Seychelles buildings is built of coral slabs; the Anglican Cathedral of St Paul; the Queen's Building, which houses the General Post Office and other government offices; the Carnegie Public Library, which contains a small, but original collection of English and French books; Gordon Square, or La Plaine, named after General Gordon of Khartoum; the old Bel Air cemetery, with its dilapidated but interesting tombs, among which is that of the corsair Jean François Hodoul; the Seychelles Hospital, with its large, homely, verandas; two fine grammar schools and the Mont Fleuri cemetery, which with its flowery shrubs and trees does not belie its name.

Satellite Tracking Station

A landmark on Mahé which can be seen from many points is the plastic-capped dome, or 'radome', of the satellite tracking station of the US Air Force. It is 100ft in diameter, is made of 830 fibreglass panels and has been designed to withstand wind velocities of up to 150 miles (240km) an hour.

The station is part of an American network engaged in outer

space research projects. It receives information from a group of research and development satellites and sends it to a central collecting point in the United States. There the information is fed into computers and compared with that from similar stations in other parts of the world. The Seychelles were chosen for the site because the islands are exactly opposite the main controlling station of the network at Sunnyvale in California, and because they are close to the Equator.

The Airport

The latest and most spectacular piece of engineering work in the Seychelles is the Colony's airport. Built of sand and other coral debris reclaimed from the sea, it is set in one of the beauty spots of Mahé, along the lovely Pointe Larue lagoon some six miles (9·6km) south of Victoria.

With an area of 250ac (100ha) and a main runway of 9,800ft (3,270m), the airport is capable of accommodating aircraft up to the size of the Boeing 747, the Jumbo Jet. The construction of the airport involved dredging and piling up to ten feet above sea level of some 3½ million cubic yards of sand and coral and the slicing off of two hill tops, which were lowered by 120ft and yielded some 100,000 cubic yards of rock and earth. Work was started in 1969 and completed in 1971.

Rochon Dam

Another important piece of engineering work carried out recently is the Rochon dam. It is six hundred feet above sea level on the Rochon river and is the first of a series of schemes which the Seychelles government has planned to provide all Mahé with a safe and plentiful water supply.

The dam consists of a 280ft long cylindrical concrete arch spanning abutments of hard Mahé granite, and its crest is 55ft above the river bed. The reservoir occupies an area of 2·3ac (1ha); has a maximum holding capacity of 11½ million gallons and is capable of yielding 0·4 million gallons of treated water per day—spectacular figures for the tiny Seychelles. It was inaugurated on

26 April 1969, almost two hundred years after the visit of the Abbé Rochon.

To the botanically minded, the small pitcher plant stand of Sans Souci is of special interest. It is the most easily accessible stand of that most curious of Seychelles plants. Situated near the Rochon dam, it can be reached by a short walk along a forest road and track.

The Beaches

Of the many lovely coral sand beaches—among the best of the world—six are outstanding. The Beau Vallon beach in south-west Mahé has a long semi-circular stretch of white sand and a fringe of takamaka trees and coconut palms. The reefless bay is one of the most beautiful of the Seychelles and from the beach there is a superb view of Silhouette and North island on the horizon. Being protected from the south-east monsoon, Beau Vallon beach and bay are particularly enjoyable from May to September and the bay is especially suitable for waterskiing. Situated about two miles ($3\frac{1}{4}$km) from Victoria, across the St Louis trans-island road, Beau Vallon is the most accessible and popular beach of Mahé and can easily be reached from Victoria by bus or taxi. It is much frequented on Sundays and other holidays and apart from the old *Hôtel des Seychelles*, with its simple and homely bungalows, it is the site of a growing number of luxury hotels which will cater for the increasing tourist trade.

The Grand'Anse beach has more rugged beauty than Beau Vallon. During fine weather (which is most of the time) it presents a colourful picture of deep-blue sea and great foaming rollers crashing on a dazzling, two mile ($3\frac{1}{4}$km) long, expanse of sand. The bay is especially suitable for surfing. It is on the west coast of Mahé, some six miles (9·5km) from Victoria across the La Misère trans-island road, and is an ideal site for picnicking.

Another lovely beach is that at North-East Bay. It has the charm of Beau Vallon, with its fringe of takamakas, casuarinas and coconut palms, and some of the savage grandeur of

Grand'Anse. It is close to Victoria at the end of about two miles (3¼km) of marine drive.

Port Launay beach, on the west coast of Mahé, is another attractive beach. Stretching along a narrow, reef-girdled bay it is one of the most peaceful beaches of Mahé, but like Beau Vallon is being turned into 'hotel land'.

Among the most secluded beaches of Mahé are those of P'tit Anse on the south-west coast, and Anse Major on the north-west coast. P'tit' Anse, which can be reached by a side-road from the Baie Lazare coastal road, is a little jewel of a beach which reminds one of a pirate's cove, while Anse Major, which can only be reached by boat or on foot on a picturesque mountain path from Bel'Ombre, is a beautiful world apart.

The Mountains

Mahé has fine mountain scenery whose beauty can be seen from the island roads, especially the trans-island ones, but it is most enjoyable during climbs to the highest peaks.

Among the roads which offer the best views of the mountains is the coastal one leading past the Cascade village, from which there is a fine view of the spectacularly carved crests overlooking the village, and the trans-island roads of La Misère and Forêt Noire which reach up to the mist belt, and give delightful views of the central massif. For the more energetic there are the climbs to Signal Hill, the Trois Frères and the Morne Seychellois, which should be undertaken with a guide.

PRASLIN ATTRACTIONS

Praslin, the second largest of the granitic islands of the Seychelles, is especially known for its coco-de-mer reserves of Vallée de Mai, Fond Ferdinand and Anse Marie-Louise. It has also some delightful coastal scenery which is best seen on foot. The walk from Côte d'Or to Anse Boudin through Anse Possession and along the beautiful Curieuse Bay is one of the most colourful of the Seychelles. But that from Grand'Anse to Petite Cour through the

Plaine Hollandaise (during which there is a breathtaking view of Cousin and Cousine island) and that from Anse Consolation to Anse Marie-Louise over a stiff rocky outcrop, are perhaps the most rewarding. To the botanically minded the walk from Baie Ste Anne through the hill coco-de-mer reserve of Fond Ferdinand, down through that of Anse Marie-Louise and back along the pretty coastal road is worth a morning's outing.

Vallée de Mai

Praslin's most impressive feature is its Vallée de Mai, a unique botanical wonder. Situated in the middle of Praslin, the Vallée de Mai is a little less than 46ac (18½ha) in area and can be reached after only a few minutes' drive on a good motor road from the villages of Grand'Anse and Baie Ste Anne.

A leisurely tour of the valley along the shady circular path takes one hour. Shorter tours may be made by the central and other paths. Landmarks in the valley include the Kiosk, which is on a knoll from which the valley can be surveyed; the tallest coco-de-mer palm which is 102ft (over 30m) high, and the luxuriantly tropical palm and pandanus grove which gives an indication of how beautiful and impressive Praslin and the whole of the Seychelles must have been originally. Closely packed in the valley are some four thousand coco-de-mer palms, which constitute a unique assembly of one of the most famous palms in the world.

Other interesting examples of the vegetation of the valley include the broad-leaved 'bois rouge', with large, strikingly red leaves and wood; 'capucin', with equally large, leathery leaves and large seeds which recall the head of a hooded capuchin monk; four other palms of the Seychelles, including the striking, noble 'palmiste' palm and the splendid 'latanier latte' palm, and three of the four endemic 'vacoas' or screwpines.

Among the creatures of the bush in the valley are emerald-green *Phelsuma* geckos; a large acavid snail which occurs only here; a rare and delicately tinted grass snake; the curious Alluaud's crab; a large, black, but reputedly harmless scorpion; the timid Seychelles tiger-chameleon; an orange-breasted flying fox; a bulbul; the beautiful and colourful Seychelles fruit, or blue pigeon and the rare Praslin black parrot.

ON SILHOUETTE

Silhouette, which is the third largest and the steepest of the granitic islands, has none of the glorious beaches of Mahé, Praslin or La Digue. It has, however, superb mountains which harbour the only true relict vegetation of the islands.

The island is of special interest to botanists and plant lovers. Among the endemic plants found on the island are five of the six endemic palms of the Seychelles, the vacoas or screwpines and the pitcher plant, of which Silhouette has the most extensive and impressive stands.

ON LA DIGUE

The fourth largest of the granitic islands, La Digue, is perhaps the most pleasing because of its green hills, its extensive swamps, which are the largest of the Seychelles, and its delightful coastal landscape. It has a relict population of paradise flycatchers, a rare bird which does not occur elsewhere in the world; the estate of l'Union, with its old plantation house and its large granitic boulder which is reputed to cover an acre, and vanilla plantations which are among the few remaining in the Seychelles.

ON THE SMALLER GRANITIC ISLANDS

Of the smaller granitic islands, three deserve to be visited. They are Frégate, Aride and Cousin. Frégate, which is the most isolated, is a delightful island on which one can have the impression of living in the old plantation days when each island was a little world of its own. The island is the home of a rare bird, the Seychelles magpie robin, which has found its last refuge there, and of the giant tenebrionid beetle. To the lover of romantic pirate stories Frégate is the island which the early eighteenth-

K

century pirates are believed to have used as one of their bases for their raids in the Indian Ocean.

Aride island, which is a few miles to the north of Praslin and owes its name to the fact that it is an almost bare, rocky, outcrop, is probably the most interesting seabird island of the Seychelles. More species of seabirds roost or breed on it than on any other island of the Colony. They include the lesser frigate, the white-tailed tropic bird and nine terns, namely the crested or swift tern, the roseate tern, the little tern, the black-naped tern, the sooty or wide-awake tern, the brown-winged or bridled tern, the common noddy, the lesser noddy and the white or fairy tern.

The tiny Cousin island off the west coast of Praslin is not only an ornithological wonder because of its intensive and almost unbelievably tame bird life, but is also one of the most unspoilt granitic islands of the Colony. It has three species of rare land birds, the brush warbler, the Seychelles foddy and the Seychelles own turtle dove, and a large population of seabirds, including some twenty thousand fairy terns and some twenty thousand wedge-tailed shearwaters.

BIRD AND DENIS ISLANDS

The two small coral islands of Bird, or Ile aux Vaches, and Denis, which are the only coral islands close to the granitic group, are also worth visiting. Bird island, the smaller of the two, is a peaceful and colourful coconut plantation during seven months of the year. From May to October it is a world of wheeling and screaming sooty terns which turn it into a great breeding fair. There is also a good fishing ground near the island.

Denis island has no bird population, but a striking landmark is its 100ft (30m) high lighthouse which peeps over the tops of the coconut palms and which is a true 'entente cordiale' product. The metallic tower of the lighthouse was constructed in France and its lighting equipment in England. It is said that when the French engineers who built the lighthouse in 1910 had completed their work, they threw the tools they had used into the sea saying that they were no longer necessary because the lighthouse would never have to be repaired. The island is especially beautiful at night when the beams of the lighthouse flash over it.

ON DESNOEUFS ISLAND

Of the many beautiful, palm-studded, outlying coral islands, one is of outstanding interest, especially to the ornithologist. It is Desnoeufs island, one of the nine main islands of the Amirantes group which is at the southern tip of the Amirantes bank. It has a huge seabird population from May to October, the breeding time of sooty terns in the Western Indian Ocean. During these months Desnoeufs presents a fantastic sight with its millions of eggs and newly-hatched terns littering the ground with millions of screaming adult birds overhead. Desnoeufs is considered to be the most important breeding centre of the sooty tern in the Indian Ocean and is a world ornithological wonder.

The sooty tern population of Desnoeufs, which was estimated to be some five million pairs in the 1930s and which, due to the overcropping of their eggs, had dropped to some 1,210,000 pairs in 1955, is on the increase again, being now of the order of some two million pairs.

12

ADVENTURES AT SEA AND SOME VISITORS

ONE of the reasons why the French reconnoitred the Seychelles from Mauritius in the first half of the eighteenth century was that they lay on the direct route to India and were navigational risks. That these risks were real, in spite of the fact that the Seychelles do not lie in the cyclone zone of the Southern Indian Ocean, is illustrated by the numerous shipwrecks which have occurred on or near the islands.

The earliest of these shipwrecks was that of the French frigate *L'Heureuse* which was lost on a reef near Providence island in 1769. The latest and also the most sensational of shipwrecks in the Seychelles waters was that of the 47,000-ton tanker *Ennerdale* of the Royal Naval Auxiliary Fleet which sank in two hours in calm weather and within sight of Mahé on 1 June 1970 after striking an uncharted granitic pinnacle. The tanker carried 20,000 tons of oil which presented a great threat to the island's beaches. The Seychelles were spared a 'Torrey Canyon' disaster by the successful dispersion of the oil as it slicked out of the wreck and later as it was released by the explosion of submarine charges.

The most dramatic of the sea adventures to have occurred in the Seychelles waters have been those concerning small boats, mostly fishing craft, which having lost sight of land during bad weather drifted haplessly for days or weeks on end before being found. Two of these stories deserve to be recalled.

The first occurred in 1891 when a small boat with the two Savy brothers and a crew of five which was crossing from Mahé to Bird island to collect sea-bird eggs was blown off its course. The boat drifted for 1,400 miles before being washed up on the coast of Arabia. By then four members of the crew were dead and the Savy brothers were unconscious. The fifth member of the crew, named L'Espoir, was carried off as a slave by Bedouins. When the Savys regained consciousness they were told by signs that they were the sole survivors. They were taken to Muscat, a month's journey by camel, and were handed to the British Resident for a reward. They returned to the Seychelles after a year's absence. The third survivor, L'Espoir, wandered in the desert with his Bedouin masters until he was stolen by a rival tribe which took him to Muscat. He, too, found his way back to the Seychelles.

The second and more dramatic of the two adventures was that of the *Marie-Jeanne*, a thirty-five feet, semi-decked boat fitted with a motor-car engine. It drifted for seventy-four days with ten people and little food or water on board before being found.

The adventure started on 31 January 1953 when Théodore Corgat, the owner of the boat, who lived on Mahé, decided to sail to Praslin to fetch a relative of a dying woman, Mrs Edith Rose. As the sea, lashed by a strong westerly wind, had been very rough during the three previous days, Corgat at first hesitated to undertake the trip. He finally consented to do so, to comply with the dying woman's wish. The boat left at 11am with Théodore Corgat, his fifteen-year-old son Selby, Coxwain Louis Laurence, the mechanic Antoine Vidot and two young men, both grandsons of Mrs Rose, Joachim Servina and Auguste Lavigne. Because of the bad weather and two minor engine breakdowns the trip, which should have taken four to five hours, took eleven.

The next morning the boat sailed back with four more passengers, namely: Mrs Ange Finesse, Mrs Georges Arissol, Jules Lavigne, a brother to Auguste, and a cook by the name of Noël Rondeau. By a curious stroke of fate Mrs Edith Rose's relative, on whose behalf the trip had been undertaken, was not on board since she had refused to sail in the rough weather, and Noël Rondeau hailed the boat to ask for passage to Mahé and came on board at the last minute with a box of mangoes and pawpaws. These fruits were to be the only food on board.

The boat had already completed more than half of the distance between Mahé and Praslin when fuel ran short and the engine stopped. The fuel tank was filled and the engine started again, but the third gear broke and clogged. As a result, the engine had to be run on the second gear which caused a higher consumption of fuel. About two miles from Mahé no fuel was left and the engine stopped once more. There was but one thing to do in the dark and windy night, to anchor and wait for the morning when the boat would be seen from the shore. However, during a strong gust of wind the anchor broke loose and the *Marie-Jeanne* began to drift. By dawn the following day she had drifted past the south end of Mahé and was heading for the open sea. Then began a long ordeal from which only two people emerged alive.

After two days of drifting there was no water left on board. On the tenth day all the food, including the skins of the fruits, had been eaten. On the thirteenth day there was a downpour and ninety litres of water were collected. On the eighteenth day a small flying fish fell on board and was shared and eaten raw. During the following eighteen days there was no food at all. On the thirty-third day a small tern landed on board. It was captured by Louis Laurence and shared. Two days later two more terns landed and were captured by Antoine Vidot. He and Selby Corgat drank their blood and their meat was shared by the other men. By then the two women were too weak to be able to eat.

In the meantime searches for the boat had been started from Mahé and when these were fruitless schooners were sent further afield towards the outlying islands. Because the currents were then pulling to the south-east the new searches were made in the region of Coëtivy. But the *Marie-Jeanne*, against all likelihood, was drifting to the south-west. These searches also failed, and a Catalina aircraft was chartered from Mombasa to search the sea further away. The *Marie-Jeanne* was not seen and all hope was given up of finding her.

On the thirty-sixth day a coral island which the people on

board believed to be Agalega appeared on the horizon. The wind was blowing towards the island and rescue appeared to be imminent. There were even tantalising views of palm trees and cottages among the coconut groves. Then the wind fell abruptly. When it blew again, it did so in the opposite direction. With make-shift oars, the men tried to row towards the island, but the island soon disappeared below the horizon. On the thirty-seventh day two large booby birds landed on board. They were captured and shared. On the thirty-ninth day another island, believed to be Providence, appeared on the horizon. This time only Théodore Corgat tried to row; the others were too weak. In desperation he tried to force the heavy and unwieldly boat towards the island. After an hour he collapsed gasping with pain and bleeding at the mouth; he had ruptured a blood vessel and was never able to stand again. Slowly the boat drifted away from the island.

Exhausted and despairing the occupants of the small boat began to die. The first to do was Mrs Ange Finesse, who was found dead on 11 March. On the forty-third day it was the turn of Mrs Georges Arissol. At the same time Louis Laurence became mad and had to be tied. On the fiftieth day Joachim Servina died. By then the survivors were so weak that they found it difficult to put the dead over the boat's side. Days and nights followed while the *Marie-Jeanne* continued to drift. On the sixty-second day Auguste Vidot died. In the evening of the same day the mad Louis Laurence jumped overboard and disappeared. On the seventieth day Théodore Corgat had a violent haemorrhage and became unconscious. Until then, although weak, he had courageously kept the boat's journal day by day providing a precious account of the boat's slow and cruel journey. When he died Auguste Lavigne and Selby Corgat were unable to put his body into the sea. They then fell into a state of intermittent unconsciousness until, on the seventy-fourth day, they heard a siren. It was that of the Italian tanker *Montallegro* which had sighted the boat. The tanker, having received no response and believing the boat to be deserted, was on the point of leaving when

Antoine Vidot managed to creep out of the small cabin and was seen. When he and Selby Corgat were taken on board the tanker they looked like skeletons. Antoine, who weighed 159lb at the beginning of the drift, weighed only 66lb. The master of the tanker, Captain Carlo Girola, sent the news of the rescue to the Seychelles and requested specialist advice from Rome on how to treat the two survivors. They were taken to Kuwait and, after treatment, returned to the Seychelles. They had been away three and a half months.

DISTINGUISHED VISITORS

Isolated from the rest of the world in the least frequented of the oceans, the Seychelles received few visitors during the first two hundred years of their history. Among the few who came, however, were some notable ones and, among the less notable, some were remarkable.

One of the most notable visitors, and the first member of the British Royal Family to have visited the Seychelles, is the Duke of Edinburgh who in October 1956, while on his way to Australia where he was to attend the Olympic Games, spent a day in the Seychelles and who as the consort of 'P'tit' Tante', which is the affectionate name under which Queen Elizabeth II is known in the Seychelles, received an enthusiastic welcome. She and the Duke of Edinburgh also paid a most successful joint visit in March 1972.

Other notable visitors have included well-known navigators and explorers, missionaries, some writers and a number of scientists. Among the navigators and explorers were La Pérouse, who on a voyage to Pondicherry called at Mahé in 1773 to shelter from bad weather; Bougainville, who came in 1775 and gave his name to Anse Bougainville on the south-west of Mahé; Admiral Laplace, who called in 1837 during his world tour on the corvette *La Favorite*; Stanley, the explorer, who on his return from Africa in 1872 missed the mail-boat at the Seychelles and had to spend a month there waiting for a ship to Aden; General Charles Gordon, who came on a military mission from Mauritius in 1881 and who designed a crest for the Colony, and Commandant Cousteau, of diving fame, who visited the Seychelles in his famous *Calypso* in 1954, 1955 and 1967.

The first notable writer to visit the Seychelles was the French poet, novelist and journalist Paul-Jean Toulet, the head of the refined Fantaisiste school and the author of the musical *Les Contrerimes*, who called in 1885 while on his way to Mauritius, and who has left the following short poem, the first ever written on the Seychelles :

'Mahé des Seychelles, le soir :
Zette est sur son dimanche,
Et sous la mousseline blanche
Brille son mollet noir.

'Les cases aux fraîches varangues
Bâillent le long des quais;
Dans les branches d'un noir bosquet
Etincellent les mangues.

'Tandis qu'en ses jardins fleuris,
Mystérieuse et belle,
Rêve une pale demoiselle
Aux chapeaux de Paris.'

The next notable literary figure to come was Henry de Monfreid, the adventurous French writer who sailed to the Seychelles in 1923 on his small boat *Altaïr*, and who gave a vivid and humorous account of his voyage in his book *La Poursuite du Kaïpan*. Compton Mackenzie came in 1946 and his novel *Mezzotint*, which was obviously inspired by the Seychelles, reflects some of the 'vieille France' atmosphere of the islands. In 1952 he was followed by Alec Waugh who told about his voyage in his book *Where the Clock Chimes Twice*. The title was suggested to him by the double-time striking clock of the Cathedral of the Immaculate Conception in Victoria. Ian Fleming, who travelled to most of the islands and who set one of his short stories, *Hildebrand's Rarity*, in the Seychelles, came in 1958.

169

THE SEYCHELLES

Expedition Visits

Because of the great attraction which the Seychelles presents to geologists, botanists and zoologists, the islands have been visited by most of the great Indian Ocean scientific expeditions of the last and present centuries, such as the German deep-sea Valdivia Expedition of 1898–9; the Percy Sladen 'Sealark' Expeditions of 1905 and 1908; the Carlsburg Foundation's Oceanographic Round the World 'Dana' Expedition of 1928–30; the John Murray 'Mabahiss' Expedition of 1933–4, the Swedish deep-sea 'Albatross' Expedition of 1947–8 and the Danish deep-sea Round the World 'Galathea' Expedition of 1950–52.

The most thorough and rewarding of these expeditions were those of the Percy Sladen Trust led by the brilliant Cambridge scientist, Professor Stanley Gardiner. A member of the second of these two expeditions was Hugh Scott, later Sir Hugh Scott, the great English coleopterist who apart from making extensive collections of Seychelles insects was also the editor of the 142 reports of the expeditions. The reports, written in English, French, German and Latin by more than a hundred distinguished specialists, were published from 1907 to 1936 in eight volumes of the Transactions of the Linnaean Society of London. They constitute the most important contribution to the natural history of the Seychelles and are a striking memorial to William Percy Sladen, the self-taught and distinguished English zoologist.

Other scientists who have visited the Seychelles include the Abbé Alexis Rochon, the French geographer and astronomer who went to the islands in the Chevalier Grenier's expedition of 1769; Pierre Sonnerat, a naturalist and sub-commissioner of Marine of the King of France, who visited the Seychelles in 1771 and who made the first scientific description of the coco-de-mer palm; Auguste Pervillé (1841), a French gardener, naturalist and traveller who made the first collection of Seychelles plants, including the striking pitcher plant; Sir Edward Newton (1867), a colonial secretary from Mauritius and distinguished ornithologist who described and named seven of the seventeen species of land birds of the Seychelles; Nicholas Pike (1871), an eminent naturalist,

American consul to Mauritius and author of *Sub-Tropical Rambles in the Land of the Aphanapterx*; Albert-Auguste Fauvel (1889), a French naturalist, traveller and distinguished sinologue, the compiler of the *Unpublished Documents on the History of the Seychelles Prior to 1810* better known as 'Le Fauvel' in Seychelles, and the author of *Le Cocotier de Mer des Iles Seychelles*, a 140-page monograph and the most complete work on the famous palm of the Seychelles.

Other visitors were Charles Alluaud, who spent two months in the Seychelles in 1892 studying the insect fauna of the islands and whose biogeographical conclusions were strikingly borne out by the results of the Percy Sladen Trust Expeditions of 1905 and 1908; Professor J. L. B. Smith, of Coelacanth fame, who visited the Seychelles in 1954 and who with his wife published the lavishly illustrated album *Fishes of Seychelles*. Among the later comers was Henry Legrand, a French lepidopterist and correspondent of the Paris Museum of Natural History, the author of the valuable monograph *Lépidoptères des Iles Seychelles et d'Aldabra* who visited the Seychelles in 1956 and in 1958 to 1960. He collected more than a hundred new species of butterflies and moths.

13   THE SEYCHELLES TODAY

FACED with demands for a higher standard of living for their growing population, the islands are now turning outwards to the world and are offering it an unspoilt, sunny natural beauty. It is hoped that tourism will improve the economy of the Seychelles and enable them to regain their financial self-sufficiency which they lost in 1958 when the Colony, for the first time in its history, became grant-aided and dependent on British government subsidies (at the rate of some £375,000 in 1971). Yet, with the recent adoption of a new constitution which provides a ministerial system of government based on the Westminster model, the Seychelles are coming of age.

Spoliation

The general appearance of the Seychelles, with the exception of the granitic islands of Praslin and Curieuse which have suffered badly from soil erosion, and the outlying coral islands of St Pierre and Assumption which have been intensively quarried for bird guano and laid waste in the process, has not changed very much over the years. However, their original unique vegetation, except in two to three square miles on the higher slopes of Mahé and Silhouette and in some secluded areas on one or two smaller islands, is gone and has been replaced by exotic species introduced by man.

Public Works

Until the 1950s there were few major constructional works in the Seychelles: the Victoria market in 1839, the Long Pier in 1848, the Le Niol reservoir in 1903, the Carnegie public library building in 1907, the new Government House in 1911, the Victoria Hospital in 1920 and the Seychelles College in 1948.

In the 1950s, with substantial Colonial Development and Welfare grants from Britain, work began to move faster. The main island roads were hard surfaced for the first time; new trans-island roads, those of La Misère and Forêt Noire on Mahé and that of Fond Boffay on Praslin, were opened and new buildings such as the Queen's Building in Victoria and the beautiful Regina Mundi Convent grammar school were constructed.

It is now in the 1970s, as if to mark the 200th anniversary of the first settlement of the islands, that the Colony is beginning to emerge from its hitherto protracted slumber. The American satellite tracking station appears to have introduced this new age. In 1969 the Rochon dam was built in the main catchment area of the central massif of Mahé. The same year also saw the start of the work for the airport which is now the pride of Mahé. The following year saw the start of another important piece of work—that of the reclamation of some 60ac (24ha) of the foreshore of Victoria, to provide a new business centre for the town and a new deep-water port for ocean-going vessels. New houses, office blocks and luxury hotels are now spreading over Mahé, and to a lesser extent over Praslin and La Digue.

Population

Like too many other developing countries the Seychelles are faced with a problem of overpopulation. It is small in world terms but is becoming acute for the tiny Seychelles.

The population of Seychelles, 2,750 in 1807, had reached 6,841 in 1851, and nearly doubled during the next twenty years. It reached 11,179 in 1871, and doubled twice during the following two forty-year periods during which it rose to the 22,691 and 41,425 in 1911 and 1960 respectively. With a birthrate of about 3·5 per cent the population is expected to reach 80,000 by the turn of this century.

The sex ratio of the population of the Seychelles, which showed a slightly higher proportion of men until 1911 (when the population consisted of 11,577 men and 11,134 women), was reversed at about that time. The ratio, which was one man to 1·05 women in 1921, has remained about the same since then. There are thus slightly more women than men in the Seychelles. This may be accounted for by the trickle of young men who, year after year, have been leaving the Colony to find work overseas.

Health

The Seychelles are free from the many infectious diseases such as malaria, yellow fever, sleeping sickness and cholera which are endemic to other neighbouring Indian Ocean territories. Justly, they have earned the reputation of being among the healthiest in the world.

Among the diseases which have presented problems in the past are leprosy, which has been practically stamped out, and tuberculosis, which flared up in recent years but was quickly brought under control.

Health problems which are still causing concern, and which are partly attributable to unsatisfactory socio-economical conditions, such as poor housing, polluted water supplies and inadequate sanitary facilities, include malnutrition (especially among infants and pregnant women), venereal diseases, among which gonorrhoea is the most prevalent, and anaemia due to a high rate of hook worm and other intestinal parasite infestations.

Education

There was scarcely any organised education in Seychelles before the second half of the nineteenth century. From 1851 onwards, however, schools were established by the Roman Catholic and Anglican churches. Until 1938 the part played by the Seychelles government in public education was limited to the inspection of schools and the payment of a modest grant-in-aid to the religious missions. With the enactment of the Education Ordinance in 1944 the government assumed the responsibility, largely through the missions which retained the ownership of their schools, for public education. The missions, especially the Roman Catholic one, are still giving invaluable help.

Today there are thirty-five primary schools, eleven junior secondary schools and two secondary grammar schools in the Seychelles, which cater respectively for nine thousand, two thousand and five hundred pupils. Of the two secondary schools, one, the Regina Mundi Convent school for girls, is owned by the Sisters of St Joseph of Cluny who came to the Seychelles in 1861, and the other, the Seychelles College for boys, is government-owned but is run and largely staffed by the Brothers of the Christian Instruction of Ploërmel. Both the convent and the college provide a five-year course leading to the Cambridge Overseas Joint School Certificate and General Certificate of Education examination. The Seychelles College also provides a two-year course leading to the Advanced level General Certificate of Education examination.

Post-secondary education in the Seychelles is provided by a government-owned Technical College which opened in 1970; by government-organised vocational courses in domestic science, pre-nursing, secretarial and student-teaching. These cater for about 300 students and the government-owned Teacher Training College has some sixty students.

Economy

As the Seychelles import a very large part of their food and all their needs in manufactured goods, their economy is based nearly as much on imports as on exports.

Although in the past non-agricultural industries, such as tortoiseshell and bird guano, have made important contributions to the life of the Seychelles, the economy will continue to be based (at least for some years to come) on two main crops, coconut and cinnamon and to a lesser extent on vanilla and patchouli.

The Seychelles can never hope to produce all their food requirements, but much larger quantities of fresh vegetables, fruits, milk and meat and other commodities like coffee, tea and lime can be produced locally to meet the demands of the growing resident

175

population and of the tourist population which is expected to reach 150,000 by 1986. The success of the tourist industry will depend on whether the Seychelles agriculture can meet this challenge.

The Future

It would appear that during the pourparlers of the Treaty of Paris which, in 1814, ceded Mauritius and the Seychelles to Britain, the United Kingdom offered to return the islands to France in exchange for the few remaining French possessions in India. The offer was declined. Had it been accepted, what would have been the fate of the Seychelles? Would they now, like Reunion island, be a proud and prosperous department of metropolitan France represented in the French National Assembly, or like the tiny St Pierre and Miquelon, a mere 'territoire d'outre-mer'? In either case the Seychelles would have now very close ties with France and closer relations with their nearest neighbour, the Malagasy Republic and the remaining French possessions of the Western Indian Ocean, from which they are completely cut off, although they have geographical, agricultural, ethnical, linguistic and cultural affinities.

The Seychelles now belong to a group of territories which are too small and poor to achieve financial independence and whose eventual relationship to Britain has yet to be defined. But the islands have much to offer the specialist visitor and the holiday-maker. Their future hopes of prosperity probably lie in the field of tourism, though the character of the Seychelles may be changed in the development process—to the regret of many who were born in the islands.

ISLAND LIST

Name	Area	Distance from Mahé

MAHÉ GROUP

Name	Area	Distance from Mahé
Mahé	36,200 acres (14,480ha)	
Ste Anne	547 acres (219ha)	Close to Mahé
Sèche or Beacon	4 acres (1·6ha)	Close to Mahé
Ronde or Round	3·4 acres (1·4ha)	Close to Mahé
Moyenne	22 acres (8·8ha)	Close to Mahé
Longue or Long	53 acres (21ha)	Close to Mahé
Cerf	314 acres (125·6ha)	Close to Mahé
Cachée or Faon	5 acres (2ha)	Close to Mahé
Anonyme	24 acres (9·6ha)	Close to Mahé
Rat or Brûlée	2 acres (0·8ha)	Close to Mahé
Sud-Est or South-East	47 acres (18·4ha)	Close to Mahé
Souris	1 acre (0·4ha)	Close to Mahé
Chauves-Souris	1 acre (0·4ha)	Close to Mahé
Ile Aux Vaches Marines	13 acres (5·2ha)	Close to Mahé
Thérèse	181 acres (72·4ha)	Close to Mahé
Conception	151 acres (60·4ha)	Close to Mahé
L'Ilot de Lislette	11 acres (4·4ha)	Close to Mahé
Ilot or North Islet	very small	Close to Mahé

SILHOUETTE GROUP

Name	Area	Distance from Mahé
Silhouette	4,000 acres (1,600ha)	14 miles (24.4km)
Nord or North	502 acres (200·8ha)	17 miles (27·2km)

PRASLIN GROUP

Name	Area	Distance from Mahé
Praslin	10,100 acres (4,040ha)	24 miles (38·4km)
Aride	97 acres (38·8ha)	29 miles (46·4km)
Ile aux Fous or Booby	very small	Close to Praslin

THE SEYCHELLES

Name	Area	Distance from Mahé
Cousin or North Cousin	71 acres (28·8ha)	Close to Praslin
Cousine or South Cousin	63 acres (25·2ha)	Close to Praslin
Curieuse	707 acres (282·8ha)	Close to Praslin
St Pierre	1·5 acres (0·6ha)	Close to Praslin
Chauve-Souris	1·5 acres (0·6ha)	Close to Praslin
Ronde or Round	51 acres (20·4ha)	Close to Praslin
La Digue	2,400 acres (960ha)	30 miles (48km)
Petite Soeur or West Sister	86 acres (34·4ha)	37 miles (59·2km)
Grande Soeur or East Sister	210 acres (84ha)	Close to La Digue
La Fouche	very small	Close to La Digue
Cocos	very small	Close to La Digue
Félicité	670 acres (268ha)	35 miles (56km)
Marianne	238 acres (95·2ha)	37 miles (59·2km)

FRÉGATE GROUP

Frégate or Frigate	504 acres (201·6ha)	32 miles (51·2km)
L'Ilot	very small	28 miles (44·8km)

MAMELLES AND RÉCIFS

Mamelles	22 acres (8·8ha)	8 miles (12·8km)
Récifs	50 acres (20ha)	17 miles 27·2km)

BIRD AND DENIS

Bird or Ile aux Vaches	174 acres (69·6ha)	52 miles (83·2km)
Denis or Oryxa	321 acres (124·8ha)	52 miles (83·2km)

PLATE AND COËTIVY

Plate	125 acres (50ha)	78 miles (124·8km)
Coëtivy	2,293 acres (917·2ha)	150 miles (240km)

AMIRANTES

African Banks or Bancs Africains	80 acres (32ha)	133 miles (218·8km)
Eagle or Rémire	66 acres (26·4ha)	135 miles (216km)
Daros	370 acres (148ha)	143 miles (228·8km)

Name	*Area*	*Distance from Mahé*
St Joseph atoll, consisting of St Joseph, Ressource, Fouquet, Benjamin, Carcassaye or Banc Ferrari, Chien, Pélican, Poules, Coco, Sable, etc.	303 acres (121·2ha)	Close to Daros
Poivre	275 acres (110ha)	152 miles (243·2km)
Ile du Sud or South	339 acres (135·6ha)	Close to Poivre
Boudeuse or King Ross	very small	197 miles (315·2km)
Etoile or Lampériaire	very small	185 miles (296km)
Marie-Louise	130 acres (52ha)	174 miles (278·4km)
Desnoeufs	86 acres (34·4ha)	180 miles (288km)
Desroches (now part of B.I.O.T.)	800 acres (320ha)	131 miles (208·8km)

ALPHONSE GROUP

Alphonse	430 acres (172ha)	223 miles (356·8km)
St François	44 acres (17·6ha)	232 miles (371·2km)
Bijoutier	very small	Close to St François

PROVIDENCE GROUP

Providence	388 acres (155·2ha)	382 miles (611·2km)
Bancs du Sud or Cerf	275 acres (110ha)	Close to Providence
St Pierre	417 acres (166·8ha)	400 miles (640km)
Farquhar, consisting of Nord, Sud, Goélette, Lapin, Milieu and Déposés (now part of B.I.O.T.)	1,994 acres (777·6ha)	430 miles (688km)

ALDABRA GROUP

Cosmoledo, consisting of Menai, Wizard or Grande Ile, Nord, Nord-Est, Pagode, Sud, etc.	1,108 acres (443·2ha)	566 miles (905·6km)
Astove	1,225 acres (490ha)	566 miles (905·6km)
Assumption or Assomption	2,735 acres (1,094ha)	622 miles (995·2km)
Aldabra (now part of B.I.O.T.)	37,824 acres (15,129·6ha)	625 miles (1,000km)

179

APPENDIX B

SELECTIVE PLANT LIST

Bois de Fer	*Vateria seychellarum* L.
Bois Rouge	*Dillenia ferruginea* (Baill.) Glg
Capucin	*Northea seychellana* Hook.
Coco-de-Mer	*Lodoicea maldivica* (Gmelin) Pers.
Fleur Paille-en-Queue	*Anagraecum brongniartianum* Bory
Jelly-fish Plant or Medusagyne	*Medusagyne oppositifolia* Bak.
Latanier Hauban	*Roscheria melanochaetes* H. Wendl.
Latanier Latte	*Verschaffeltia splendida* H. Wendl.
Manglier de Grand Bois	*Randia sericaea* L.
Palmiste	*Deckenia nobilis* H. Wendl.
Pitcher Plant	*Nepenthes pervillei* L.
Takamaka	*Calophyllum inophyllum* L.
Vacoa Marron	*Pandanus Seychellarum* L.
Vacoa Parasol	*Pandanus hornei* L.
Vanille Sauvage	*Vanilla phalaenopsis* Mill.

180

Name – Farquhar after Sir Robt. T. Farquhar
1st Br. Gov of Mauritius 1824. Previously
Joao de Nova from Galicia. Joined Sey. in 1832
Chevalier Desroches, Gov Isle de France
et Bourbon 1771
Denis de Trobriand in L'Etoile 1777
took possession

Position   4 – 5° S, 55 – 56° E for main
granite islands. They are less than
600 mls north of Madagascar, 1,000 miles
east of Kenya and 1750 miles west of
Bombay
Denis Is. 50 mls north of Mahé, Aldabra
600 mls. south west
Silhouette is 3rd largest island & has peak
of 2,600 ft.
Mahé rises to nearly 3,000 ft.
Coëtivy – largest sand cay 100 mls
south of Mahé added 1908

Colony originally consisted of the
granite islands (continental) with the
three coral Bird & Denis to N, & Plate Is
to So.
Praslin 24 mls N. of Mahé (he
was Gov. of Fr. East India Co.)

Ocean area nearly ½ million Sq. miles
Total area 110 Sq. miles
40 high granite islands or rocks
45 coral atolls or islets – less than ½
 ~ 25 sq miles – fish   inhabited
       guano
Granite islands arise   copra
 continental mass from submerged
       250 ft. below Sea level
Mahé – pop 45,000; in Victoria 13,000
6,000 on Praslin, La Digue. Silhouette 1,000
Low coral – 1000 – 1,500 (varies)

climbing & pitcher plant

Flora & Fauna — 6 unique pines (thirty up at Dales

80 plants that grow nowhere else
1,200 insects found " " else
6 very rare birds (Jelly-fish plant small tree

Mammals — orange-breasted flying fox
& two small bats

Bird Sanctuaries & colonies sp. Cousin
Aldabra & Desnoeufs (Amirantes)

Giant Tortoises — all gone from Mahé 180

Isle des Vaches — dugong — Bird Is
mermaids gone

Coco-de-mer — only on Praslin & Curieuse
aphrodisiac. Market in So. India,
Saturated by Fr. buccaneer 1769 Jan
First reported by Magellan's Survivor
Gen Charles Gordon 1881 | Tree of Knowledge
100 ft tall. leaves
Span 20 ft. Seed
take 7 yrs to mature
Biggest seeds known 35 l

Many birds in danger
Nile crocodiles (caimans) extinct since 185
Anse " on La Digue

Giant Tortoise — now very rare on Seychel
Aldabra. 5 ft long 500 lbs.. One (James)
handed over at Surrender of Mauritius w
in British Museum

Chameleons
Caecilians, or vers de terre like earth-worm
6 unique types
Green Turtle & Hawkesbill turtle greatly reduced
Sail fish — can be 25 ft. long
? Indonesians → Madagascar 1,800 yrs ago
Casuarina tree
Arabs 600–950 AD
on Madagascar Mauritius 975 AD Tombs
Silk

Ancient map   18 May 1971
Airport   38 June 71
Rare funds   24 July 72

27 Ap 1970   Bicent St Anne
                20c 50c 85c, 350

KE $\overline{VII}$ 1903 Crown CA +
1906 Multip Crown C

G $\overline{V}$ 1912 as QV + KEd. Postage Posta

1917 Type 2 Mult Crown

1921 " " Mult Script
12c + 1R Die

S.J. $\llcorner$ 6 May 35 12c extra flagstaff mast

1 Jan 1938 K.G. $\overline{VI}$ — Chalky. Change
in Aug 41
+ 10/2/38
1R + 5R.

— 1952 3 Nov. Death-like 5c Ed. Crown +
Crown missing

1956 15 Nov Pierre de Possession

1961 11 Dec. Centenary of 1st PO

1962 21 Feb Views definitives

1867 18 Sept Univ. Suffrage

1968 Human Rights 2 Sept. Drs Day Hayward

1868 30 Dec. PRASLIN — 200 YRS

6 - 25 March '68 Local Handstamps (Seg.
Postage
P° 100
23mm. circle fancy

1969 ? Sept Man on Moon (22 July

— 1969 3 Nov. 5c. PICAAULT landing 1742
15c Konigsberg II not?
20c RN refuelling in mid
30c. Pierre de Possess
60c. Corsairs
1R. de Quincy capital
5R
1R 50 Sibille - Chiffone
3R 50 Duke Ed 1956

SELECTIVE ANIMAL LIST

Bare-Legged Scops Owl	*Otus insularis* (Tristram)
Black Parrot	*Coracopsis nigra barklyi* (Newton)
Blue or Fruit Pigeon	*Alectroenas pulcherrima* (Scopoli)
Broad-billed Bulbul	*Hypsipetes crassirostris* (Newton)
Brush Warbler	*Bebrornis sechellensis* (Oustalet)
Caecilians	*Hypogeophis* spp.
Crocodile	*Crocodylus niloticus* Gray
Flying Fox	*Pteropus seychellensis seychellensis* Milne-Edwards
Foddy	*Foudia sechellarum* (Newton)
Giant Tenebrionid Beetle	*Pulposipes herculaeanus* Solier
Giant Tortoise	*Testudo gigantea* (Schweigger)
Green Geckos	*Phelsuma* spp.
Kestrel	*Falco area* (Oberholser)
Leaf Insects	*Phyllium* spp.
Magpie Robin	*Copsychus sechellarum* (Newton)
Paradise Flycatcher	*Terpsiphone corvina* (Newton)
Red-headed Turtle Dove	*Streptopelia picturata rostrata* (Bonaparte)
Sooty or Wideawake Tern	*Sterna fuscata nubilosa* Sparmann
Sun Bird	*Nectarinia dussumieri* (Hartlaub)
Tiger Chameleon	*Chamaeleo tigris* Kuhl

BIBLIOGRAPHY

The works are listed under separate chapters. Where the name of an author is given followed by a figure in brackets, the latter denotes the chapter under which the work is first listed.

CHAPTER 1

AVEZAC, M. D' and FROBERVILLE, E. DE. *Iles de l'Afrique*. L'Univers, Vol 6, Part 3, Paris 1848

BAKER, B. H. *Geology and Mineral Resources of the Seychelles Archipelago*. Memoir No 3, Geological Survey of Kenya (Nairobi 1963)

DORAISWAMY, Iyer and FRANCIS, K. A. The Climate of Seychelles with Special Reference to its Rainfall. *Memoirs of the India Meteorological Department, 27 (1941), 45–59*

FRYER, J. C. F. The Structure and Formation of Aldabra and Neighbouring Islands with Notes on their Flora and Fauna. *The Transactions of the Linnaean Society of London, 2nd Series Zoology, 14 (1911), 397–441*

LIONNET, J. F. G. Names of the Islands. *Atoll Research Bulletin* 136 (1970), 221–4

MILLER, J. A. and MUDIE, J. D. Potassium-Argon Age Determinations on Granite from the Island of Mahé in the Seychelles Archipelago. *Nature 192 (1961), 1174–1175*

PIGGOTT, C. J. *A Soil Survey of Seychelles*. Technical Bulletin No 2, Land Resources Division, Directorate of Overseas Surveys, Ministry of Overseas Development, Tolworth 1968

SCOTT, H. General Conclusions Regarding the Insect Fauna of the Seychelles and Adjacent Islands. *The Transactions of the Linnaean Society of London, 2nd Series Zoology, 19 (1933), 307–391*

WEGENER, A. *The Origin of Continents and Oceans*. Translated from the Fourth Revised German Edition by John Biram with an Introduction by B. C. King (1966)

183

BIBLIOGRAPHY

CHAPTER 2

BAILEY, H. Palmae Sechellarum. *Gentes Herbaram, 6 (1942), 1–48, Ithaca New York*

BOLIVAR, I. and FERRIÈRE, C. Orthoptera, Phasmidae of the Seychelles. *The Transactions of the Linnaean Society of London, 2nd Series Zoology, 15 (1912) 293–300*

DUROCHER YVON, F. Seychelles Botanical Treasure : The Coco-de-Mer Palm (*Lodoicea maldivica* Pers.) *La Revue Agricole de l'Ile Maurice, 26 (1947), 68–87*

FAUVEL, A. A. *Unpublished Documents on the History of the Seychelles Anterior to 1810.* Seychelles 1909

FAUVEL, A. A. Le Cocotier de Mer des Iles Seychelles. *Annales du Musée Colonial de Marseille, 3rd Series, 1 (1915), 1–307*

GAYMER, R. D. T., BLACKMAN, R. A. A., DAWSON, P. G., PENNY M. J. and PENNY, C. MARY *The Endemic Birds of Seychelles. Ibis, III (1969), 157–176*

GEBIEN, H. Coleoptera, Heteromera : Tenebrionidae. *The Transactions of the Linnaean Society of London, 2nd Series Zoology, 18 (1922), 261–324*

LIONNET, J. F. G. The Vallée de Mai and the Coco-de-Mer Palm. *Principes, 9 (1966), 134–138*

LIONNET, J. F. G. *The Romance of a Palm: Coco-de-Mer.* Seychelles 1970

MOINE, J. Histoires de Crocodiles. *Journal of the Seychelles Society, 3 (1963), 65–67*

RAWLINS, R. R. The General in the Garden. *Blackwood's Magazine, 280 (1956), 1–10*

SCOTT, H. (1)

VESEY-FITZGERALD, D. On the Vegetation of Seychelles. *Journal of Ecology, 27 (1940), 465–483*

CHAPTER 3

CHIOVENDA, E. La Culla del Cocco. *Webbia, 5 (1921–23), 199–294, 359–449*

EDMONSON, C. H. Viability of Coconut Seeds after Floating in the Sea. *Occasional Papers of the Bernice P. Bishop Museum, 16 (1941), 293–304*

HEYERDAHL, T. *The Kon-Tiki Expedition by Raft Across the South Seas.* Translated from the Norwegian by F. H. Lyon. London 1950

LINDSAY, H. A. Kon-Tiki : A Mare's Nest. *Walkabout, 21 (1955), 35–36*

McEWEN, A. C. Fragments of Early Seychelles History. *Journal of the Seychelles Society, 1 (1961), 17–21*

SAUER, J. D. *Plants and Man on the Seychelles Coast.* Madison and London 1967

TOUSSAINT, A. *History of the Indian Ocean.* Translated from the French by June Guicharnaud (1966)

CHAPTER 4

AVEZAC, M. D' and FROBERVILLE, E. DE (1)

BRADLEY, JOHN T. *The History of Seychelles.* Vol 1. Seychelles 1940

DAYER, P. LOUIS *Les Iles Seychelles. Esquisse Historique.* Fribourg 1967

FAUVEL, A. A. (2)

FOSTER, W. Journal of John Jourdain, 1608–1617, Describing His Experiences in Arabia, India and the Malay Archipelago. *Hakluyt Society Works, 2nd Series, 16 (1905), 1–394*

McEWEN, A. C. (3)

ROCHON, A. M. DE *Voyage a Madagascar et aux Indes Orientales.* Paris 1791

SAUER, J. D. (3)

SPRAY, WILLIAM A. British Surveys in the Chagos Archipelago and Attempts to Form a Settlement at Diego Garcia in the late Eighteenth Century. *The Mariner's Mirror, 56 (1970), 59–76*

WEBB, A. W. T. *Story of Seychelles.* Seychelles 1964

CHAPTER 5

DAYER, P. LOUIS (4)

FAUVEL, A. A. (2)

LY-TIO-FANE, M. *Mauritius and the Spice Trade: The Odyssey of Pierre Poivre.* Port Louis 1958

185

M

BIBLIOGRAPHY

Ly-Tio-Fane, M. l'établissement du Jardin du Roi Aux Seychelles. *Journal of the Seychelles Society, 6 (1968), 25–31*

Ly-Tio-Fane, M. *Mauritius and the Spice Trade: The Triumph of Jean Nicolas Céré and His Isle Bourbon Collaborators.* Paris and The Hague 1970.

CHAPTER 6

Barkly, F. A. *From the Tropics to the North Sea. Five Years in Seychelles.* London 1890

Bradley, John T. (4)

Dayer, P. Louis (4)

Edinburgh, hrh the duke of *Birds from Brittania.* London 1962

Fauvel, A. A. (2)

Fescourt, M. *Histoire de la Double Conspiration de 1800.* Paris 1819

Lenôtre, G. *Les Derniers Terroristes.* Paris 1932.

Pelly, J. On the Island of Mahé, Seychelles. *The Royal Geography Society, 35 (1865), 231–237*

Webb, A. W. T. (4)

CHAPTER 7

Benedict, B. *People of the Seychelles.* London 1966

Jones, J. S. The French Patois of the Seychelles. *African Affairs, 51 (1952), 237–247*

Jourdain, E. *Du Français aux Parlers Créoles.* Paris 1956

Sylvain, S. *Le Creole Haïtien. Morphologie et Syntaxe.* Thèse Honorée du Diplôme de l'Ecole des Hautes Etudes à la Sorbonne. Wetteren 1936

Webb, A. W. T. *Population Census 1960.* Seychelles 1961

CHAPTER 8

Anonymous *Minutes of the Seychelles Legislative Council Meetings of 1st February 1951, 21st June 1951 and 29th April 1952.* Seychelles 1951, 1952

Bradley, John T. (4)

DAYER, P. LOUIS (4)

GREENE, W. *Official Status and Rights of the Roman Catholic Church in Mauritius, as Shown by the Laws of the Colony.* Port-Louis 1883

HANCHETT, DIANE E. *Report on the Teaching of English and French in Primary and Secondary Schools in the Seychelles Islands, 1967.* Appendix X, Annual Report of the Department of Education for the year 1969. Seychelles 1970

TOUSSAINT, A. La Langue Française a l'Ile Maurice. *Revue Française d'Histoire d'Outremer, 56 (1969), 398–427*

WEBB, A. W. T. (4)

CHAPTER 9

ANONYMOUS *Notes Statistiques sur les Iles Seychelles.* Mauritius 1850

BAKER, B. H. (1)

DAVIDSON, G. BINDLEY American Trade in the Indian Ocean (1795–1815). *Journal of the Seychelles Society, 3 (1963), 1–10*

DUROCHER YVON, F. The Coconut Industry of Seychelles. *World Crops, 5 (1953), 437–441*

HORNELL, JAMES *The Turtle Fisheries of the Seychelles Islands.* London 1927.

LIONNET, J. F. G. Seychelles Vanilla. *World Crops, 10 (1958), 441–444; 11 (1959), 15–17*

LIONNET, J. F. G. Seychelles Cinnamon. *World Crops, 13 (1961), 259–262*

LIONNET, J. F. G. Seychelles Patchouli. *World Crops, 14 (1962), 336–338*

PARSONS, JAMES J. *The Green Turtle and Man.* Gainesville 1962

TOUSSAINT, AUGUSTE Shipbuilding in Seychelles. *Journal of the Seychelles Society, 5 (1966), 29–40*

TOUSSAINT, AUGUSTE *La Route des Iles. Contribution à l'Histoire Maritime des Mascareignes.* Paris 1967

VESEY-FITZGERALD, D. Review of Biological Control of Coccids on Coconut Palms in the Seychelles. *Bulletin of Entomological Research 44 (1953), 405–413*

WEBB, A. W. T. *Agricultural Census 1960.* Seychelles 1961

WEBB, A. W. T. (4)

187

BIBLIOGRAPHY

CHAPTER 10

BRADLEY, JOHN T. (4)

FARMER, H. V. *Seychelles Postage Stamps and Postage History.* London 1955

RASSOOL, ROBERT SHAPHEE Collecting Seychelles Stamps. *Journal of the Seychelles Society, 5 (1960), 41–51*

SONNERAT, PIERRE *Voyage à la Nouvelle Guinée.* Paris 1776

TOULET, PAUL-JEAN *Vers Inédits.* Paris 1936

WAUGH, ALEC *Where the Clock Chimes Twice.* London 1953

CHAPTER 11

RIDLEY, THE HON M. W. and PERCY, LORD RICHARD. *The Exploitation of Sea Birds in Seychelles.* London 1958

CHAPTER 12

ANGELIN, P. *Le 'Marie-Jeanne' Sur l'Océan Indien.* Seychelles 1966

FAUVEL, A. A. (2)

FLEMING, IAN *For Your Eyes Only. The Hildebrand's Rarity.* London 1960

LEGRAND, HENRY Lépidoptères des Iles Seychelles et d'Aldabra. *Mémoires du Muséum National D'Histoire Naturelle de Paris, Series A, Zoology,* 37 (1965) 1–210

MACKENZIE, COMPTON *Mezzotint.* London 1961

MOMFREID, HENRY DE *La Poursuite du Kaïpan.* Paris 1934

PIKE, NICHOLAS *Sub-Tropical Rambles in the Land of the Aphanapteryx.* London 1873

SMITH, J. L. B. and SMITH, M. M. *Fishes of Seychelles.* Grahamstown 1963

SONNERAT, PIERRE *Voyage à la Nouvelle Guinée.* Paris 1776

TOULET, PAUL-JEAN *Vers Inédits.* Paris 1936

WAUGH, ALEC *Where the Clock Chimes Twice.* London 1953

CHAPTER 13

HOSSEN, P. *Report of the Medical Department for the Years 1968–69.* Seychelles 1970

BIBLIOGRAPHY

JOHNS, A. W. *Annual Report of the Education Department for the Year 1969*. Seychelles 1970

SPITZ, A. J. W. Health and Morbidity Survey, Seychelles 1956–57. *Bulletin of the World Health Organisation, 22 (1960), 439–467*

ACKNOWLEDGEMENTS

The author gratefully acknowledges his indebtedness to the persons listed in the bibliography and to his many friends, too numerous to mention, who have expressed interest in the book and have offered encouragement about it.

INDEX

INDEX

194

195

INDEX

199

INDEX